EUROPE

A vineyard and lavender fields in southern France

The World in Maps
EUROPE

Martyn Bramwell

Lerner Publications Company • Minneapolis

**First American edition published in 2000
by Lerner Publications Company**

© 2000 by Graham Beehag Books

Lerner Publications Company
A division of Lerner Publishing Group
241 First Avenue North
Minneapolis, MN 55401 U.S.A.

Website address: www.lernerbooks.com

Library of Congress Cataloging-in-Publication Data

Bramwell, Martyn.
 Europe / by Martyn Bramwell
  p. cm. — (The world in maps)
 Includes index.
 Summary: Presents information about the location, topography, climate, population, industries, language, and currency of each of the European countries.
  ISBN 0-8225-2913-0 (lib. bdg.)
 1. Europe—Juvenile literature. 2. Europe—Maps—Juvenile literature.
 [1. Europe.] I. Title. II. Series: Bramwell, Martyn. The world in maps.
 D1051. B73 2000
 940—dc21   99-006944

Printed in Singapore by Tat Wei Printing Packaging Pte Ltd
Bound in the United States of America
1 2 3 4 5 6 – OS – 05 04 03 02 01 00

Picture credits
Page 14 top Nowegian Tourist Board
Pages 16 Finnish Tourist Board
Page 17 Swedish Travel & Tourism Council
Page 20 Tourism Flanders
Page 24 Switzerland Tourism

CONTENTS

0°

Arctic
Circle

ATLANTIC

OCEAN

Norwegian
Sea

SWEDEN

NORWAY

North

Sea

White
Sea

Gulf of Bothnia

FINLAND

Lake
Onega

Lake
Ladoga

REP. OF
IRELAND

UNITED
KINGDOM

NETHERLANDS

BELGIUM

LUXEMBOURG

Bay of
Biscay

DENMARK

GERMANY

Baltic Sea

ESTONIA

LATVIA

LITHUANIA

(RUSSIA)

BELARUS

POLAND

Oder

Vistula

UKRAINE

Dniester

FRANCE

Loire

Seine

SWITZERLAND

A L P S

Danube

CZECH
REP.

AUSTRIA

SLOVENIA

CROATIA

SLOVAKIA

HUNGARY

ROMANIA

MOLDOVA

ANDORRA

Adriatic Sea

BOSNIA-
HERZEGOVINA

SERBIA
and
MONTENEGRO

BULGARIA

Black Sea

PORTUGAL

SPAIN

Balearic Is.

Corsica

Sardinia

ITALY

MACEDONIA

ALBANIA

GREECE

40°

Mediterranean Sea

Sicily

Malta

Crete

6

0°

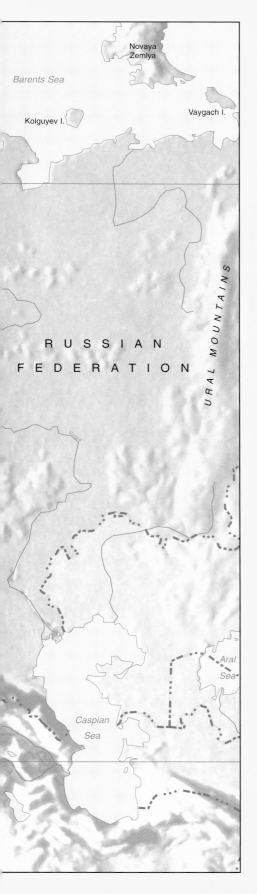

EUROPE

Europe is the second-smallest continent, yet it contains 40 independent countries. If you traveled the 925 miles from London, England, to northern Bosnia-Herzegovina, you would cross 10 countries each with its own history, traditions, and culture—that's 10 countries in the distance between Chicago, Illinois, and New Orleans, Louisiana.

With so many diverse **nationalities** packed into such a small land area, Europe has had a turbulent history. Over the past 2,000 years, great empires have come and gone. New countries have emerged, and old ones have disappeared. National borders have been redrawn time after time as a result of wars, alliances, and treaties.

Europe's landmass stretches 4,000 miles east to west and slightly more than 3,000 miles north to south. An abundance of bays, **fjords**, peninsulas, and inland seas have created a coastline that is nearly 38,000 miles long. The continent has a wide range of climates, soil types, resources, and scenery. It is one of the most densely populated and most productive regions in the world.

Europe has had an immense influence on the world despite its small size. Beginning in the fourteenth century, Europeans expanded their culture through art, music, science, medicine, navigation, industry, and technology. Intellectuals conceived many new ideas about economics, politics, and social justice. The world changed dramatically after World War II (1939–1945). Many European countries were devastated—their cities, industries, farms, and transport systems in ruins. It took many years to repair the damage. The United Kingdom, France, the Netherlands, and Belgium were also weakened by the loss of overseas territories as, one after another, their former colonies became independent nations. The United States and the Soviet Union emerged from the war as the world's superpowers.

Modern Europe continues to change. The former Soviet Union has fragmented into a dozen separate countries. But as one group separates, another develops. Major European countries have joined together as the European Union (EU, formerly the European Community). Its aim is to bring the people of Europe closer together culturally, technologically, and financially.

The European Union (EU)
The European Union has 15 independent states—Austria, Belgium, Denmark, Finland, France, Germany, Greece, Ireland, Italy, Luxembourg, the Netherlands, Portugal, Spain, Sweden and the United Kingdom.

The organization's aims are to bring the people of Europe closer together, to promote economic and social progress, and to make the voice of Europeans heard on the international scene. In March 1998, the EU began a process that will lead to the admittance of 13 more states—Bulgaria, Cyprus, the Czech Republic, Estonia, Hungary, Latvia, Lithuania, Malta, Poland, Romania, Slovakia, Slovenia, and Turkey.

Portugal and Spain

Portugal

Status:	Parliamentary Democracy
Area:	35,514 square miles
Population:	10 million
Capital:	Lisbon
Language:	Portuguese
Currency:	Portuguese escudo
	(100 centavos)

Overseas Territories
Azores—Eastern Atlantic Ocean
Madeira—Eastern Atlantic Ocean

Situated on the westernmost edge of the European continent, Portugal is 350 miles north to south and about 125 miles wide. It covers roughly one-sixth of the Iberian Peninsula, which it shares with its neighbor, Spain. The self-governing islands of the Azores and Madeira in the eastern Atlantic are all that remain of Portugal's once-vast overseas empire.

Northern Portugal is mountainous, with a mild damp climate and a short dry season. Farmers use the poor upland soil mainly for grazing sheep and goats and the forests for producing lumber and wood pulp. The hotter, drier, southern coastal plains are an area of flatland rising inland to the **meseta**—a region of dry highlands cut by broad river valleys. Portugal's most fertile land is found in the valleys and on the coastal plains.

Farmers grow mostly grains—corn in the north and wheat in the south. Other crops include beans for local use and olives, grapes, limes, oranges, and almonds for export. Portugal exports nearly half the world's supply of cork, as well as wine, turpentine, resin, and Atlantic sardines.

Portugal's main mineral resources are tungsten ore, copper ore, and coal. Lisbon and Setúbal have shipbuilding and repair yards, and the manufacturing centers around Lisbon and Porto produce processed food, leather goods, ceramics, glass, and textiles.

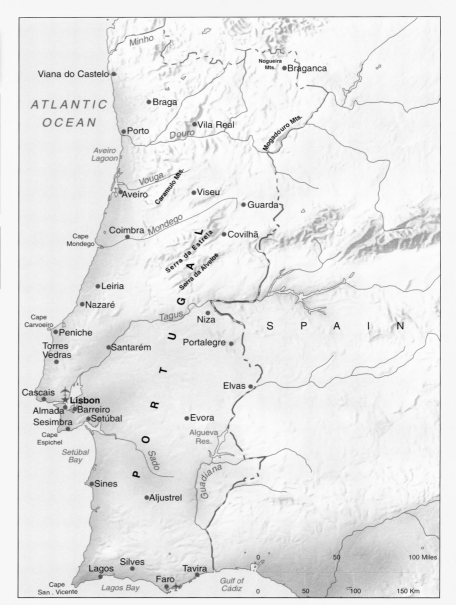

Southern Portugal's Algarve coast extends for 60 miles from Cape San Vicente eastward to Faro. Tourists flock to its sandy beaches, coves, and spectacular rock formations. Quiet villages, farmland, and medieval towns provide plenty to explore farther inland.

Spain

Status:	Parliamentary Monarchy
Area:	195,363 square miles
Population:	39.4 million
Capital:	Madrid
Language:	Spanish
Currency:	Peseta (100 céntimos)

Overseas Territories
Canary Islands—Eastern Atlantic Ocean
Ceuta—North coast of Morocco
Melilla—North coast of Morocco

One of the oldest occupied territories in Europe, Spain has been inhabited for more than 100,000 years. Dry, scrub-covered meseta, lying at 2,000 to 2,500 feet above sea level, covers most of the central region. Numerous mountain ranges run across the middle of the country and along the north and south coasts. Prime farmland is found on the coastal lowlands of Valencia and Alicante, in the Ebro River Valley, and in the Guadalquivir Basin.

The inland climate is hot and dry in summer and cold in winter. Meseta farmers graze sheep and goats and grow barley and oats. Forestry workers produce lumber, cork, and resin. Farmers in the cool damp northern regions and in the warm mild Mediterranean coastal areas produce wheat, barley, fruits, sugar beets, vegetables, cotton, and tobacco. Olive groves and vineyards cover vast expanses. Spain is the world's primary olive producer and one of the world's leading wine makers.

Tourism contributes a great deal to the economy. Visitors flock to the country's Mediterranean coast, to the historic inland towns, and to the Balearic and Canary Islands. The northern cities of Bilbao, Santander, and Oviedo house the country's iron and steel, shipbuilding, automobile, chemicals, and cement industries. Spaniards mine copper, lead, zinc, silver, mercury, and other metals. Barcelona is the main center for manufactured goods such as textiles, electronics, leather goods, and food processing.

Left: Spain has a daily routine all its own. Most people work until midday, take a three-hour break, then work again until seven. The evening meal is seldom eaten before 10 P.M., and there's still time to sit and talk or to enjoy the country's wealth of traditional dances.

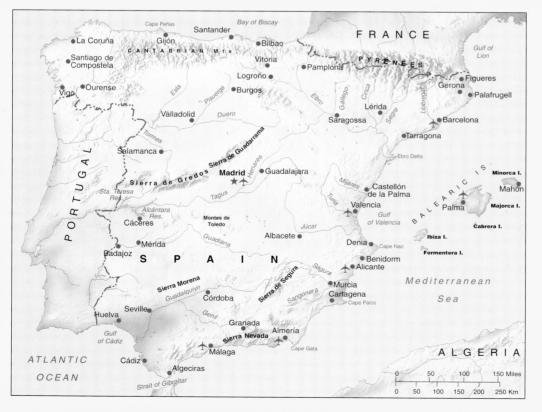

Above: Antonio Gaudi's spectacular Church of the Holy Family is one of many architectural attractions in Barcelona, Spain's second-biggest city. Barcelona is also the country's principal seaport, a center of trade and industry, and a world-famous cultural center.

France

France

Status:	Parliamentary Democracy
Area:	212,934 square miles
Population:	59.1 million
Capital:	Paris
Language:	French
Currency:	Franc (100 centimes)

Overseas Territories
French Polynesia—Mid-Pacific Ocean
St. Pierre and Miquelon—Off
  Newfoundland, Canada
Mayotte—Indian Ocean, off Madagascar
Wallis and Futuna Is.—Western Pacific
  Ocean
New Caledonia—Western Pacific Ocean
Kerguelen—Southern Ocean

Overseas Departments
Guadeloupe—Caribbean
Martinique—Caribbean
French Guiana—South America
Réunion—Indian Ocean

Above: Among the great attractions of Paris are the city's hundreds of sidewalk cafés, where tourists and local residents alike can relax and talk and watch the world go by.

Right: The village of Dieulefit lies in the Rhône Valley in south central France. Local farmers plant crops in the valley's fertile soils, and vines thrive on the hillsides.

France is one of the largest countries in Europe, extending about 600 miles north to south and 600 miles east to west. Fertile plains and rolling hills dominate northern France. The hard granite moors of Brittany jut into the Atlantic Ocean. The capital city of Paris stands in the middle of a huge saucer-shaped hollow called the Paris Basin. The city is home to the Cathedral of Notre Dame, the Eiffel Tower, and the Louvre. Western France is covered in flat plains, rimmed with sandy beaches that attract tourists to the Atlantic coast. Most of France's inland borders are mountainous. The Pyrénées separate France from Spain in the southwest. To the southeast, the Alps form a barrier between France and its neighbors Switzerland and Italy. The lower wooded Vosges and Ardennes Mountains mark France's borders with Germany and Belgium in the east and northeast.

France's **Massif Central** boasts beautiful scenery, opulent chateaus, and three of the country's great rivers—the Loire, the Seine, and the Rhône. Several large industrial centers (Clermont-Ferrand, Limoges, St. Étienne, and Lyon) have developed where these rivers flow into the northern lowlands. France's other important industrial centers lie near Paris, in the Nord-Pas-de-Calais and Lorraine coalfields, and close to the ports of Le Havre and Dunkerque on the English Channel. France has to import most of its coal and oil, but 70 percent of the country's power derives from its nuclear power plants. Mountain rivers and the world's largest tidal power station, at the mouth of Brittany's Rance River, supply energy for France's surging hydroelectric power.

France is the world's fourth-ranked industrial nation—following the United States, Japan, and Germany. The country produces vast quantities of steel and aluminum and is a leading manufacturer of cars, locomotives, aircraft, turbines, and other machinery. Electrical goods, chemicals, pharmaceuticals, and textiles comprise the remainder of its industrial exports. France is also Europe's leading agricultural nation. Sixty percent of the land supports crops and livestock. Northern farmers produce grains, beets, beef, veal, poultry, and dairy products. Mediterranean farmers grow fruits and vegetables. Many French tend grapes to make wine.

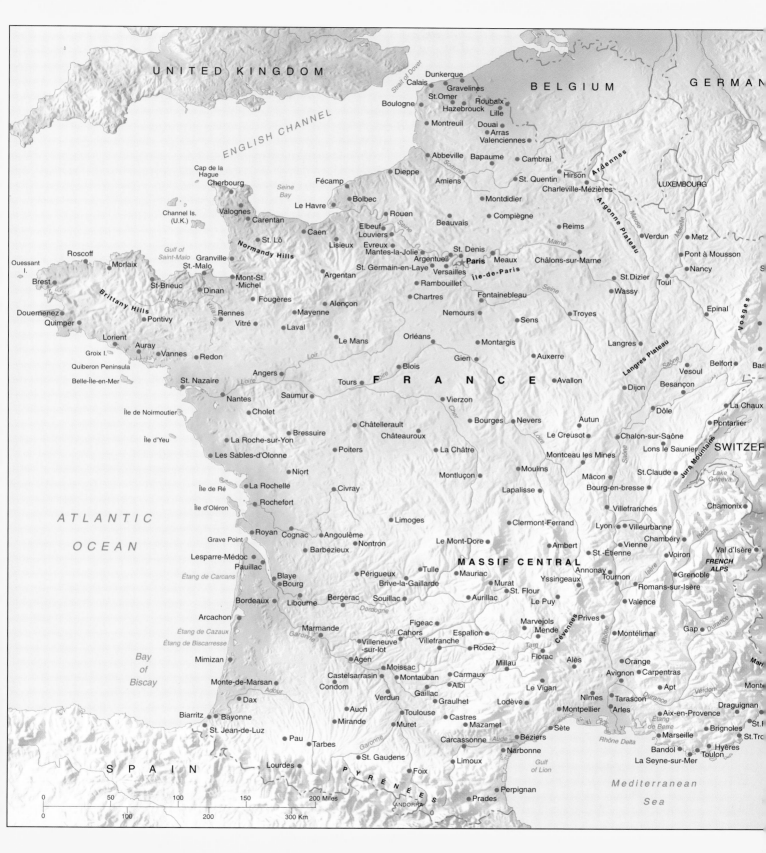

UNITED KINGDOM

BELGIUM

GERMAN

LUXEMBOURG

ENGLISH CHANNEL

Strait of Dover

Dunkerque
Calais
Gravelines
St.Omer
Roubaix
Boulogne
Hazebrouck
Lille
Montreuil
Douai
Arras
Valenciennes

Abbeville
Bapaume
Cambrai
Somme
Hirson
Ardennes
Dieppe
Amiens
St. Quentin
Charleville-Mézières

Fécamp
Rouen
Beauvais
Compiègne
Reims
Verdun
Metz

Argonne Plateau
Meuse
Moselle

Cap de la Hague
Cherbourg
Seine Bay
Le Havre
Bolbec
Elbeuf
Louviers
Montdidier

Valognes
Carentan
Seine
Evreux
Mantes-la-Jolie
St. Denis
Argenteuil
Paris
Meaux
Châlons-sur-Marne
Marne
Pont à Mousson
Nancy

Channel Is. (U.K.)
St. Lô
Caen
Lisieux
St. Germain-en-Laye
Versailles
Île-de-Paris
St.Dizier
Toul

Ouessant I.
Roscoff
Morlaix
Gulf of Saint-Malo
Granville
St.-Malo
Normandy Hills
Argentan
Rambouillet
Chartres
Fontainebleau
Seine
Wassy
Epinal
Vosges

Brest
St-Brieuc
Mont-St.-Michel
Dinan
Rance
Fougères
Alençon
Nemours
Troyes
Langres

Douernenez
Quimper
Brittany Hills
Pontivy
Vitré
Rennes
Vilaine
Laval
Mayenne
Sens
Langres Plateau
Saône
Belfort
Bas

Lorient
Auray
Vannes
Redon
Angers
Le Mans
Orléans
Montargis
Auxerre
Vesoul
Besançon

Groix I.
Quiberon Peninsula
Belle-Île-en-Mer
St. Nazaire
Nantes
Saumur
Loire
Tours
FRANCE
Blois
Gien
Avallon
Dijon
Dôle
La Chaux
Pontarlier

Île de Noirmoutier
Cholet
Vierzon
Cher
Bourges
Nevers
Autun
Le Creusot
Chalon-sur-Saône
Lons le Saunier
SWITZER

Île d'Yeu
Bressuire
Châtellerault
Châteauroux
La Châtre
Loire
Montceau les Mines
Mâcon
St.Claude
Jura Mountains

La Roche-sur-Yon
Poitiers
Moulins
Bourg-en-bresse
Lake Geneva

Les Sables-d'Olonne
Niort
Montluçon
Lapalisse
Villefranches
Chamonix

Île de Ré
La Rochelle
Civray
Limoges
Clermont-Ferrand
Lyon
Villeurbanne

Île d'Oléron
Rochefort
ATLANTIC OCEAN
Royan
Cognac
Angoulême
Nontron
Le Mont-Dore
Ambert
St.-Étienne
Chambéry
Isère
Val d'Isère
FRENCH ALPS

Grave Point
Barbezieux
MASSIF CENTRAL
Annonay
Vienne
Voiron
Grenoble

Lesparre-Médoc
Périgueux
Tulle
Mauriac
Yssingeaux
Tournon
Romans-sur-Isère

Pauillac
Étang de Carcans
Blaye
Bourg
Brive-la-Gaillarde
Murat
St. Flour
Le Puy
Valence

Bordeaux
Libourne
Bergerac
Souillac
Aurillac
Dordogne
Marvejols
Mende
Privas
Gap
Durance

Arcachon
Étang de Cazaux
Marmande
Figeac
Cahors
Villefranche
Rodez
Cévennes
Rhône
Montélimar

Mimizan
Étang de Biscarrosse
Garonne
Villeneuve-sur-lot
Agen
Moissac
Millau
Florac
Alès
Orange
Avignon
Carpentras
Apt
Mart

Bay of Biscay
Monte-de-Marsan
Castelsarrasin
Condom
Montauban
Carmaux
Albi
Le Vigan
Nîmes
Tarascon
Aix-en-Provence
Draguignan

Dax
Verdun
Gaillac
Graulhet
Lodève
Montpellier
Arles
St.

Biarritz
Bayonne
Auch
Toulouse
Castres
Mazamet
Sète
Béziers
Marseille
St.Tro

St. Jean-de-Luz
Mirande
Muret
Garonne
Carcassonne
Narbonne
Aude
Rhône Delta
Bandol
Hyères
Toulon

Pau
Tarbes
St. Gaudens
Limoux
Gulf of Lion
La Seyne-sur-Mer

SPAIN
Lourdes
PYRÉNÉES
Foix
Prades
Perpignan
Mediterranean Sea

ANDORRA

SWITZER
Étang de Berre
Brignoles

50   100   150   200 Miles
100   200   300 Km

United Kingdom and Ireland

United Kingdom

Status:	Constitutional Monarchy
Area:	94,548 square miles
Population:	59.4 million
Capital:	London
Languages:	English, Welsh, Gaelic
Currency:	British pound (100 pence)

The United Kingdom of Great Britain and Northern Ireland comprises a group of islands separated from mainland Europe by the English Channel, the Strait of Dover, and the North Sea. England, Scotland, the principality of Wales, and Northern Ireland comprise the country's four political divisions.

The United Kingdom's landscape is quite varied. Mountains and **moors** dominate the north. Rolling hills and fertile plains cover the southern and eastern lowlands. The rugged peaks and calm mountain lakes of the Scottish Highlands, England's Lake District, and Snowdon in northern Wales attract many tourists. Upland farmers graze sheep on the high ground and grow grain, hay, and **fodder crops** at the lower elevations. Depending on soil and climate, farmers grow wheat, barley, oats, vegetables, peas, beans, sugar beets, fodder crops, and fruit. Large dairy and beef herds graze on the rich lowland pastures. Agriculture employs only 1 percent of the country's workforce, but farming is highly mechanized and very productive.

The United Kingdom's early economy depended on heavy industries such as coal mining, steel, machinery, automobiles, chemicals, textiles, and pottery. Industrial centers developed in northern England and Scotland, in the western Midlands, and near the ports of London, Liverpool, Glasgow, and Belfast. Modern manufacturing such as light engineering, electrical goods, computers, biotechnology, and food processing have developed in parts of the United Kingdom where the older industries have declined. Although the country's imports exceed its exports, the economy is bolstered by banking, by insurance, by other financial services, and by tourism.

United Kingdom Overseas Territories

Anguilla—Caribbean
Bermuda—Western Atlantic Ocean
British Antarctic Territory—Antarctica
British Indian Ocean Territory—Indian Ocean
British Virgin Islands, Cayman Islands, Montserrat, Turks and Caicos Islands—Caribbean
Falkland Islands—South Atlantic Ocean
Gibraltar—Mediterranean
Pitcairn, Henderson, Ducie, and Oeno Is—South western Pacific Ocean
St. Helena, Ascension, Tristan da Cunha—Southeastern Atlantic Ocean
South Georgia and South Sandwich Is—South Atlantic Ocean

Above: Like New York, London has an instantly recognizable skyline—especially dramatic in the evening sun.

Republic of Ireland

Status:	Republic
Area:	27,135 square miles
Population:	3.7 million
Capital:	Dublin
Languages:	English, Gaelic
Currency:	Irish pound (100 pence)

Southern Ireland's lush green countryside and rich pastures have earned the country its famous nickname—the Emerald Isle. Separated politically from Northern Ireland in 1921, southern Ireland first became the Irish Free State. In 1949 it was renamed the Republic of Ireland (Eire in Gaelic).

The central part of the country is low-lying, with peat bogs and clusters of low rounded hills called **drumlins**. Low rugged mountains rise to about 2,500 feet in the north and west. Southwestern Ireland's long ridges of hard sandstone jut out to sea like fingers, creating long sea inlets and natural harbors. Ireland's hills, lakes, and coastal scenery attract many visitors each year.

Nearly 70 percent of the country is farmland. Atlantic winds carry plenty of rain, and the climate is cool and mild. Farmers raise large dairy herds in the country's southern and midland regions. Smaller herds of beef cattle graze in the east and west. Primary crops are wheat, oats, potatoes, and sugar beets. Farmers also grow barley for cattle feed and to make beer. The Irish enjoy excellent fishing opportunities and export fish, lobster, prawns, and shellfish. Ireland's manufactured goods include machinery, textiles, fine glassware, and electronic equipment. The island's main manufacturing center is a vast government-supported industrial estate near Shannon airport.

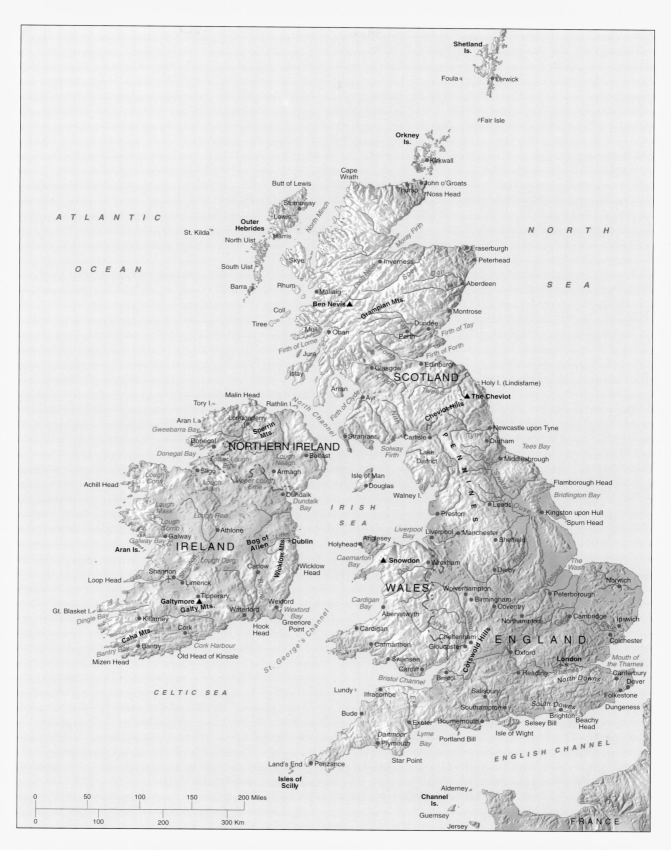

Shetland
Is.

Foula • Lerwick

• Fair Isle

Orkney
Is.

• Kirkwall

Cape
Wrath
John o'Groats
Butt of Lewis • Thurso • Noss Head
Stornoway
Lewis
Outer
Hebrides • Fraserburgh
St. Kilda North Uist Moray Firth Inverness • Peterhead
Harris Spey Don
South Uist Skye Aberdeen
Barra Mallaig
Rhum Ben Nevis ▲ Grampian Mts. Montrose
Coll Dundee
Tiree Mull Oban Perth Firth of Tay
Firth of Lorne Firth of Forth
Jura Glasgow • Edinburgh
Islay SCOTLAND Holy I. (Lindisfarne)
Arran Tweed
Malin Head Ayr ▲ The Cheviot
Tory I. Rathlin I. Cheviot Hills
Aran I.a Londonderry North Channel Carlisle Newcastle upon Tyne
Gweebarra Bay Sperrin Stranraer Durham Tees Bay
Donegal Mts. Solway Lake Middlesbrough
Donegal Bay Lough Firth District
Neagh Isle of Man Flamborough Head
Sligo Armagh Douglas Bridlington Bay
Achill Head Lough Lough Dundalk Walney I. Leeds Ouse
Conn Erne Upper Lough Dundalk Preston Kingston upon Hull
Lough Erne Bay Liverpool Spurn Head
Mask Lough IRISH Bay Anglesey Liverpool Manchester
Lough Ree SEA Sheffield
Galway Corrib Athlone Holyhead ▲ Snowdon Derby
Galway Bay IRELAND Bog of Wicklow Caernarfon Wrexham The
Aran Is. Allen Dublin Bay Wash
Lough Derg Carlow Wicklow Dee WALES Wolverhampton Welland
Shannon Head Cardigan Birmingham Norwich
Loop Head Limerick Bay Aberystwyth Coventry Peterborough
Tipperary Wexford Cambridge
Gt. Blasket I. Galtymore ▲ Waterford Wexford Cardigan Northampton Ipswich
Galty Mts. Bay Carmarthen ENGLAND Colchester
Dingle Bay Killarney Greenore Gloucester Cotswold Oxford
Caha Mts. Cork Hook Point Swansea Cheltenham Hills London
Bantry Bay Bantry Head Cardiff Reading Thames Canterbury
Mizen Head Cork Harbour Bristol North Downs Dover
Old Head of Kinsale Bristol Channel Salisbury Folkestone
CELTIC SEA Lundy Southampton South Downs Beachy
Ilfracombe Brighton Head
Bude Selsey Bill Dungeness
Exeter Bournemouth
Dartmoor Lyme Portland Bill Isle of Wight
Plymouth Bay ENGLISH CHANNEL
Land's End Penzance Star Point
Isles of
Scilly Alderney
Channel
Is. Guernsey
FRANCE
Jersey

ATLANTIC

OCEAN

NORTH

SEA

St. George's Channel

0 50 100 150 200 Miles
0 100 200 300 Km

13

Norway and Denmark

Norway

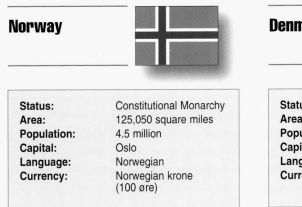

Status:	Constitutional Monarchy
Area:	125,050 square miles
Population:	4.5 million
Capital:	Oslo
Language:	Norwegian
Currency:	Norwegian krone (100 øre)

Denmark

Status:	Constitutional Monarchy
Area:	16,637 square miles
Population:	5.3 million
Capital:	Copenhagen
Language:	Danish
Currency:	Danish krone (100 øre)

Danish Overseas Territories
Greenland—North Atlantic Ocean
Faeroe Islands—North Atlantic Ocean

Below: Norway's fjords—very deep sea inlets—were gouged out by glaciers flowing from the mountains into the sea. They provide the country with one of the most spectacular coastlines in the world.

Norway stretches 1,100 miles north to south, but its coastline has so many bays, headlands, and **fjords** that the country's shoreline is more than 2,100 miles long. The northernmost third of the country lies inside the Arctic Circle, and Hammerfest is Europe's most northerly city. In midsummer, northern Norway sees nearly 24 hours of daylight, giving the country the nickname of Land of the Midnight Sun. More than 150,000 small islands, rocks, and reefs are scattered along Norway's Atlantic coast.

Norway is a mountainous country, and 80 percent of it is more than 500 feet above sea level. The only area of lowland occurs around Oslo in the south. Because Norway has few large **alluvial plains,** Norwegian farms average only about 40 acres. Farmers grow barley and potatoes and raise pigs, beef, and dairy cattle. The climate is cool in summer and cold in winter, but some farmers are able to grow fruit trees on sunny hillsides.

Forestry and fishing are Norway's traditional industries, but the country's abundant hydroelectric power has enabled Norwegians to build many manufacturing plants. Modern industries include lumber and wood pulp, metal goods, paper, processed food, engineering parts, and ship and boat building. Norway also has one of the world's largest merchant shipping fleets. Norway's already high standard of living grew after the country discovered oil and gas fields beneath the North Sea in the 1960s. The country's most significant industry is now the production and export of oil and natural gas.

Nearly surrounded by water, Denmark consists of the low-lying Jutland Peninsula and 482 islands. The country's only link to the mainland is its 43-mile-long border with Germany that runs across the neck of the peninsula. Most Danes live on Sjaelland, Fyn, Lolland, Falster, and Bornholm, but about 100 of the smaller islands are also inhabited.

Nearly 70 percent of Denmark's land area is given over to agriculture. Danish farmers best utilize their fertile soils and mild climate by concentrating on high-value food products such as butter, cheese, bacon, and ham. Most farmers grow barley, green fodder crops, and root crops—used chiefly for animal feed. About 60 percent of the country's food production is exported as meat and dairy products, mainly to the United Kingdom and Germany. Fishing fleets based in West Jutland and on Greenland and the Faeroe Islands catch sand lances, cod, herring, and Norway pout. Factories in Jutland process much of the catch for export.

Denmark's only natural resources are oil and gas from beneath the North Sea and granite and kaolin (a fine white clay) from the quarries on Bornholm. Industrial centers around Copenhagen and other big cities import raw materials, turning them into lucrative products such as machinery, food-processing equipment, silverware, furniture, textiles, chemicals, and pharmaceuticals.

Right: Merchants' houses line the quay (docks) in the port area of Copenhagen, whose Danish name—København—translates as "merchants' harbor."

0   100   200   300 Miles

0   100   200   300   400   500 Km

NORWEGIAN

SEA

NORTH

SEA

North Cape
Kjelvik
Berlevåg   Båtsfjord
Sørøya   Hammerfest   Lebesby   Hamningberg
Kistrand   Vadsø
Vanna I.   Polmak   Varanger
Ringvassøy I.   Alta   Fjord
Kvaløy I.   Tromsø   Karasjok   Kirkenes
Skibotn
Finnsnes   RUSSIA
Vesterålen
Hadsel   Harstad
Vågan   Narvik
Svolvær
Lofoten   Vest Fjord
Sørfold
Bodø   Roghan
Beiarn

Mo

Vega   Mosjøen
Brønnøysund   Grane
Vikna   Kjølen Mts.
Folda Fjord   Grong   FINLAND
Namsos   Snåsa
Frøya I.   Steinkjer
Levanger
Trondheim   SWEDEN
Kristiansund   Halsa
Surnadalsøra
Ålesund   Sunndalsøra
Stranda   Røros
Norddal   NORWAY
Dombås
Dovre Mts.
Sande   ▲
Galdhøpiggen
Fåberg
Voss   Lillehammer
Myrdal   Fagernes
Bergen   Gjøvik   Hamar
Uskedal   Kongsvinger
Skjold   Dalen   Drammen   ★ Oslo
Haugesund
Stavanger   Horten
Bygland   Larvik   Fredrikstad
Evje   Sarpsborg
Egersund   Arendal
Kristiansand
Mandal   Skagerrak

Gulf of Bothnia

Åland

Gulf of Finland

ESTONIA
Hiiumaa
Saaremaa
Gotland   Gulf of
Riga
Öland
LATVIA
BALTIC SEA
LITHUANIA

Hjørring
Jammer Bay
Lim Fjord   Ålborg
Nissum Bay   Ålborg
Viborg   Bay
Holstebro   Randers
Ringkøbing   Silkeborg
Århus
DENMARK   Horsens
Esbjerg   Copenhagen
Fanø I.   Odense   SJAELLAND
Main I.   FYN   BORNHOLM
Rømø I.   Svendborg   Rønne
LOLLAND   FALSTER   (RUSSIA)

GERMANY   POLAND

Kattegat

Sweden and Finland

Sweden

Status:	Constitutional Monarchy
Area:	173,730 square miles
Population:	8.9 million
Capital:	Stockholm
Language:	Swedish
Currency:	Swedish krona (100 øre)

Finland

Status:	Republic
Area:	130,560 square miles
Population:	5.2 million
Capital:	Helsinki
Languages:	Finnish, Swedish
Currency:	Markka (100 penniä)

Sweden is a land of beautiful lakes, snow-covered mountains, and rushing water. The country's population is small compared to its land area, and Swedes enjoy a very high standard of living. Northwestern Sweden's mountainous terrain is dotted with hundreds of small **glaciers**. A broad, forested plateau sloping down from the mountains to the Gulf of Bothnia dominates northeastern Sweden. Hydroelectric power stations perched on the plateau's many rivers provide more than 60 percent of Sweden's energy. High-voltage power lines carry the electricity to the industrial areas of central and southern Sweden. The remainder of Sweden's energy is from nuclear power stations, but Sweden has decided to phase out nuclear energy by 2010.

A broad low-lying region of woodlands and lakes stretches across southern Sweden from Göteborg to the capital city of Stockholm. Natives and tourists flock to this area to camp, hike, and fish. Much of Sweden's manufacturing industry is located around Göteborg in the west and Stockholm and Eskilstuna in the east. Vast reserves of iron ore, copper, gold, lead, and other metals cover much of the Inner Northland. The country is a leading exporter of iron and steel, cars, aircraft, ball bearings, electrical equipment, and household appliances. Sweden also boasts the world's second-largest shipbuilding industry. Other important exports include chemicals, lumber, wood pulp and paper, textiles, and food products.

Swedish agriculture is concentrated in the fertile lowlands at the country's southern tip. Modern, highly mechanized farms specialize in meat and dairy produce. Farmers grow barley, oats, and hay for animal feed and grains, fruits, and vegetables for human consumption.

Finland's capital, Helsinki, lies farther north than any other capital city except Reykjavík, the capital of Iceland. Most of Finland is low and flat. Two-thirds of the country is below 650 feet. Finland's highest point—in the far northwest—is only 4,357 feet above sea level.

Finland has three principal landscapes—the Upland District, the Lake District, and the flat Coastal Lowlands. Peat bogs and forests of pine, spruce, and birch cover the northern uplands, giving way to treeless Arctic **tundra** in the far north. Very few people other than the nomadic Sami (also called the Lapps), along with their reindeer herds, live this far north. South central Finland is a lowland region of bogs, dense forests, and more than 60,000 lakes. Almost one-tenth of the country is covered by water. The lakes are shallow and fill the hollows in the thick layer of clay left behind by ice age glaciers. Coastal plains, 40 to 80 miles wide, extend along the Gulf of Bothnia and the Gulf of Finland.

Finland's forestry workers provide lumber, plywood, wood pulp, and paper for export. The country also mines copper, nickel, iron, zinc, chromium, and other useful metals. Engineering and shipbuilding are Finland's second-largest industries, followed by glass, chemicals, and textiles. Farmers on the coastal lowlands raise dairy and beef cattle, poultry, and pigs. They also grow wheat, barley, and vegetables.

Below: The land around Finland's Saimaa Lake

Map Scale:

0 — 100 — 200 — 300 Miles
0 — 200 — 400 Km

NORWEGIAN SEA

BARENTS SEA

RUSSIA

NORWAY

SWEDEN

FINLAND

Utsjoki

Inarijärvi

Lotta

Enontekiö

Kiruna

Kittilä

Sodankylä

Vittangi

Torne

Pelkosenniemi

Gällivare

Ounasjoki

Torne

Rovaniemi

Jokkmokk

Övertorneå

Kemijoki

Kemi

Boden

Tornio

Kalix

Luleå

Kulle

Sorsele

Arvidsjaur

Piteå

Hailuoto

Oulu

Oulujoki

Oulujärvi

Dikanäs

Storuman

Skellefte

Skellefteå

Raahe

Kajaani

Vuokatti

Lycksele

Åsträsk

Lövånger

Vilhelmina

Dorotea

Hällnäs

Pyhäjärvi

Sukeva

Iisalmi

Alanäs

Hoting

Bygdeå

Umeå

Kokkola

Jakobstad

Hotagen

SWEDEN

Kuopio

Outokumpu

Offerdal

Gäxsjö

Ådalsliden

Nykarleby

Joensuu

Östersund

Örnsköldsvik

Vaasa

Lapua

Åsarna

Håsjö

Krämfors

Seinäjoki

Varkaus

Indals

Härnösand

Jyväskylä

Klövsjo

Kaskinen

Linsell

Ljusnan

Sundsvall

Ljusdal

Gnarp

Sysma

Lillhärdal

Los

Hudiksvall

Tampere

Heinola

Särna

Pori

Bollnäs

Söderhamn

Rauma

Hämeenlinna

Kouvola

Mora

Höljes

Rättvik

Gävle

Forssa

Lahti

Anjalankoski

Leksand

Falun

Gävle Bay

Hyvinkää

Kotka

Appelbo

Borlänge

Åland

Naantali

Turku

Porvoo

Klar

Västerdal

Helsinki

Ärvika

Kopparberg

Uppsala

Ekenäs

Gulf of Finland

Karlstad

Västerås

Mariehamn

Hangö

Karlskoga

Örebro

Eskilstuna

Stockholm

Hiiumaa

L. Peipus

Strömstad

Vänern

Katrineholm

Södertälje

ESTONIA

Motala

Norrköping

Saaremaa

Uddevalla

Lidköping

Linköping

Gotland

Gulf of Riga

Trollhättan

Gränna

Göteborg

Boras

Huskvarna

Västervik

LATVIA

Mölndal

Jönköping

Visby

Vetlanda

Målilla

Eman

Varberg

Växjö

Borgholm

Halmstad

Kalmar

Öland I.

Tingsryd

LITHUANIA

Helsingborg

Karlskrona

Kalmar Sound

BALTIC SEA

Malmö

Kristianstad

Hanö Bay

Ystad

Bornholm

Trelleborg

(RUSSIA)

GERMANY

POLAND

BELARUS

Kattegat

Gulf of Bothnia

Top: Stockholm, Sweden's beautiful capital city, extends over 14 islands, linked by almost 50 bridges.

Above: The midnight sun

17

Estonia, Latvia, Lithuania

Estonia

Status:	Parliamentary Democracy
Area:	17,413 square miles
Population:	1.4 million
Capital:	Tallinn
Languages:	Estonian, Russian
Currency:	Estonian kroon (100 cents)

Latvia

Status:	Parliamentary Democracy
Area:	24,942 square miles
Population:	2.4 million
Capital:	Riga
Languages:	Latvian, Russian
Currency:	Lat (100 santimes)

Lithuania

Status:	Parliamentary Democracy
Area:	25,174 square miles
Population:	3.7 million
Capital:	Vilnius
Languages:	Lithuanian, Russian
Currency:	Litas (100 cents)

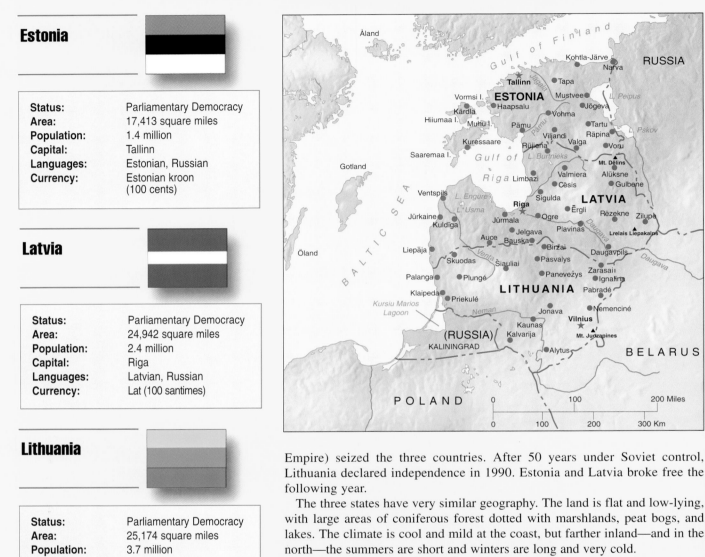

The three small countries known as the Baltic States—Estonia, Latvia, and Lithuania—cluster along the eastern shore of the Baltic Sea. Russia, Belarus, Poland, and the small territory of Kaliningrad—part of the Russian Federation—border the countries on the inland side. Before World War I (1914–1918), the Baltic States belonged to the Russian Empire. When the war ended in 1918, the three states gained independence. In 1940 during World War II, the Soviet Union (a successor to the Russian Empire) seized the three countries. After 50 years under Soviet control, Lithuania declared independence in 1990. Estonia and Latvia broke free the following year.

The three states have very similar geography. The land is flat and low-lying, with large areas of coniferous forest dotted with marshlands, peat bogs, and lakes. The climate is cool and mild at the coast, but farther inland—and in the north—the summers are short and winters are long and very cold.

Estonia's main resources are oil shale, which provides fuel for power plants, and phosphates, which are used to make fertilizer and other chemical products. Shipbuilding, engineering, chemicals, and textiles are the country's primary industries.

Latvia produces telephones and other electronic equipment, railroad cars, machinery, and household appliances. The country has no coal, oil, or gas reserves and imports most of its energy supplies from Estonia.

Lithuania has some oil and gas and a large nuclear power plant near the town of Ignalina. The country imports crude oil, processing it into fuels and other chemical products. Lithuania's factories produce industrial machinery, ceramics, glass, and textiles.

All three countries have fishing fleets and forest-based industries that create lumber, wood pulp, paper, and wood products such as furniture. Farmers in the Baltic States raise beef and dairy cattle, pigs, sheep, and poultry. Essential field crops are rye, oats, sugar beets, potatoes, and other vegetables. Most farmers grow fodder crops, and many specialize in growing flax, which is used to make linen and linseed oil.

The Netherlands

The Netherlands—historically known as Holland—is one of Europe's smallest countries and is also one of the most crowded. Each square mile of land supports almost 1,200 people, compared to 277 per square mile in France and 76 per square mile in the United States. Despite this high **population density**, the Dutch people have one of the highest standards of living in Europe. International trade, many diverse industries, and a very efficient farming system all help support excellent state-funded education, health, and social services. And the population gets a lot of exercise—there are as many bicycles as there are people in the Netherlands.

Nearly one-third of the country's land area is below sea level. The highest point, Vaalser Berg in the Southern Uplands, rises to just 1,053 feet above sea level. This lack of elevation has led people to name the Netherlands and neighboring Belgium the Low Countries. The country's southern delta region is formed by the Maas, Rhine, and Schelde Rivers, which empty into the North Sea. Huge earth-filled dams, called dykes, prevent the North Sea from flooding vast areas of reclaimed land called **polders**. Dutch engineers are world leaders in land reclamation and in designing flood and sea defenses.

Farms occupy nearly 70 percent of the Netherlands, and farmers concentrate on high-value produce such as butter and cheese, flower bulbs, and tomatoes and other vegetables grown in greenhouses. Potatoes, sugar beets, and wheat grow in some areas.

The Netherlands has both oil and natural gas but imports large quantities of crude oil to feed the large refineries at Rotterdam. Imported raw materials support the manufacturing industries clustered around the busy ports of Amsterdam and Rotterdam—the gateways to Europe's inland waterways. Factory workers produce chemicals, vehicles, electrical and electronic equipment, fine china, pottery, and a wide range of food products.

The Netherlands

Status:	Constitutional Monarchy
Area:	15,768 square miles
Population:	15.8 million
Capital:	Amsterdam
Language:	Dutch
Currency:	Guilder (100 cents)

Overseas Territories
Aruba—Caribbean
Netherlands Antilles—Caribbean

Top: Tulip fields and windmills—the most typical of all Dutch scenes

Above: More than 100 canals wind through Amsterdam, adding to the charm of this historic capital city.

Belgium

Belgium

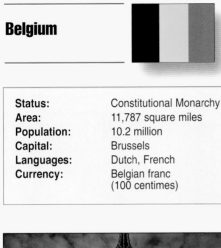

Status:	Constitutional Monarchy
Area:	11,787 square miles
Population:	10.2 million
Capital:	Brussels
Languages:	Dutch, French
Currency:	Belgian franc (100 centimes)

Above: A carpet of flowers decorates the Grand' Place (main square) in Brussels, the Belgian capital. The square is lined with ornate houses built in the 1600s for the city's merchant and craft guilds (associations).

Right: In military cemeteries across the Belgian lowlands, thousands of immaculately tended graves witness the tragic losses of two world wars.

Belgium, like the Netherlands, is densely populated and enjoys a high standard of living. Most of the country is flat and low-lying, rising gently to the forested hills of the Ardennes region on Belgium's borders with France and Luxembourg. Reclaimed polders along the coast provide the best cropland, while farmers in the higher inland regions concentrate on livestock and dairy farming. Belgium's main crops are wheat, barley, oats, sugar beets, flowers, vegetables, and hops (used to make the country's famous beers).

Excellent roads, railroads, and waterways link Belgium's manufacturing areas with Europe's main trading ports in the Netherlands. Belgian industries import raw materials for production of exports, such as textiles, glassware, metal goods, and electrical products. Luxury goods include lace and chocolate. Eighty percent of Belgium's energy is nuclear power, one of the highest percentages in the world.

Belgium was a founding member of the EU. Many of the EU's governing bodies are headquartered in the capital city of Brussels alongside the command center of the North Atlantic Treaty Organization (NATO) and other international organizations.

Germany

Germany

Status:	Federal Republic
Area:	137,830 square miles
Population:	82 million
Capital:	Berlin
Language:	German
Currency:	Deutsche mark (100 pfennigs)

Germany is among the world's leading trade nations, is a major international finance center, and is one of the most powerful partners in the EU. Before World War II, Germany was a single country, but at the end of the war the Allied Powers—Britain, France, the United States, and the Soviet Union—divided it in two. The Federal Republic of Germany (West Germany) remained allied with western Europe, while the German Democratic Republic (East Germany) became part of the Communist bloc, controlled by the Soviet Union. The two German states were reunited after the East German people rejected Communism in 1990. But reunification has not been easy.

Western Germany's industry is modern and efficient, and the people have long enjoyed a very high standard of living. By contrast, eastern Germany's industries were badly run-down and inefficient. Roads, utilities, hospitals, and other services were seriously diminished, and the standard of living was low. Since reunification, Germany is investing a great deal of money in eastern Germany's modernization, but the process will take many years.

Germany lacks abundant natural resources. Large coal deposits lie beneath the western Ruhr Valley—the country's main industrial region—and small oil and gas fields dot the northern lowlands, but Germany imports most of its necessary raw materials and energy. The country's economic strength rests on modern industries turning out high-quality manufactured goods such as automobiles, trucks, trams and buses, machine tools, printing presses, precision instruments, and electronic equipment. Germany also exports many chemical and pharmaceutical products.

Northern Germany is a flat lowland plain with patches of fertile farmland and sandy **heathland.** Farmers grow barley, oats, rye, potatoes, and sugar beets. Central Germany consists of rolling uplands and small, fertile river valleys, where farmers concentrate on producing grapes (for wine) and hops (for beer). Cattle, pigs, horses, poultry, and sheep graze throughout the country, but Germany's best pastureland is in the southeast. In southern Germany the land rises toward the spectacular Alps. Forested mountains, beautiful lakes, picturesque castles, and medieval towns full of decorative half-timbered buildings draw thousands of tourists to southern Germany each year.

Above: Koblenz, on the Rhine River, is one of Germany's oldest and most beautiful cities. Most of the old town center was destroyed in World War II but has been painstakingly restored into a major tourist attraction.

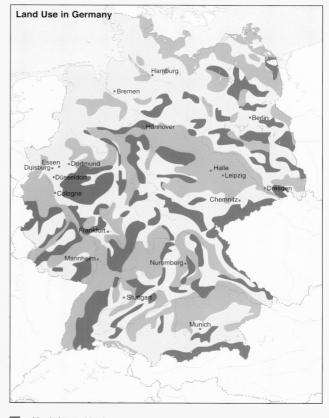

Land Use in Germany

Hamburg
Bremen
Berlin
Hannover
Essen
Duisburg
Dortmund
Düsseldon
Halle
Leipzig
Cologne
Dresden
Chemnitz
Frankfurt
Mannheim
Nuremberg
Stuttgart
Munich

■ Mostly forested land

Mostly cropland

Grazing land mixed with cropland

● Major urban-industrial center

21

Germany

Right: The magnificent Brandenburg Gate stands in the center of Berlin. Before the Berlin Wall was built close by in 1961, the gate was the city's principal east-west crossing point. When the wall came down, thousands flocked to the Brandenburg Gate to celebrate.

Right: The Rhine is one of Europe's most important rivers. It rises in the Swiss Alps and winds for 820 miles across northern Europe, finally emptying into the North Sea. Its valley contains some of Germany's most beautiful scenery and most spectacular castles.

Below: Heidelberg, on the Neckar River in southern Germany, is a beautiful old university city overlooked by a sixteenth-century castle.

Switzerland and Austria

Switzerland

Status:	Federal Republic
Area:	15,942 sq. miles
Population:	7.1 million
Capital:	Bern
Languages:	German, French, Italian
Currency:	Swiss franc (100 centimes)

Switzerland is a small, landlocked country in the center of western Europe. Mountains cover nearly three-fifths of the land. The snowcapped Alps in the south include 15,203–foot Monte Rosa and the dramatic 14,691–foot Matterhorn. The forested Jura Mountains rise in the north to 5,518 feet. Most Swiss people live on the Mittelland—a central plateau of rolling hills, broad river valleys, and beautiful lakes such as Lake Geneva, Lake Lucerne, and Lake Constance.

Switzerland is poor in natural resources. Mountain rivers provide hydroelectric power, but all other fuels and industrial raw materials must be imported. The Swiss have made up for this lack of resources by specializing in the production of high-quality, high-value precision-engineering goods such as clocks and watches, machine tools, scientific instruments, microscopes, and laboratory equipment. Swiss factories also produce glassware, textiles, chemicals, pharmaceuticals, and luxury foods such as chocolate and cheese. Switzerland spends more on imports than it earns from its exports but makes up the difference with a thriving tourist industry—nearly 12 million visitors a year—and the country's world-famous international banking and insurance businesses.

Farmers in the more fertile valleys grow grains, potatoes, sugar beets, vegetables, and fruit. Many farmers also raise beef and dairy cattle. Those in the south take advantage of their nearness to the mountains, grazing their animals on the high alpine pastures in the summer and herding them back to the sheltered valleys for the winter.

Top: Bern, the Swiss capital, lies on the Aare River.

Center: Schönried is a typical Swiss alpine village, surrounded by mountain pastures at 4,000 feet above sea level.

Bottom: The twin towers of Zurich's Grossmünster Church overlook the old city, the Limmat River, and Lake Zurich.

Austria

Status:	Federal Republic
Area:	32,378 sq. miles
Population:	8.1 million
Capital:	Vienna
Language:	German
Currency:	Austrian schilling (100 groschen)

The jagged Austrian Alps and their foothills cover most of western, southern, and central Austria. At 12,470 feet, the Grossglockner towers over this mountainous area. Central Europe's longest river—the Danube—flows through northern Austria's fertile valleys and past the forested hills that border the Czech Republic. Eastern Austria is a broad fertile plain that slopes gently eastward and merges with the great plain of Hungary.

Austria's farmers utilize only about 20 percent of the land, but modern methods and machinery allow them to meet three-quarters of the country's food needs. Meat and dairy production, grains, sugar beets, potatoes, fruits, and vegetables contribute to both the local and export markets. Forests cover about 40 percent of the country. Strict conservation laws control lumber companies, allowing them to produce a steady but replaceable supply of sawed lumber, pulp, and paper.

Graphite, magnesite, and iron ore are Austria's most valuable mineral resources, but local miners also excavate copper, zinc, lead, and salt. Hydroelectricity generated by mountain rivers accounts for two-thirds of Austria's energy needs. The balance derives from imported fuels and small local oil and gas fields. Most of the manufacturing industries are located in the Danube Valley and around Vienna, where factories produce iron and steel, automobiles, tractors, machinery, electrical goods, plastics, chemicals, textiles, ceramics, and processed foods. Like most alpine countries, a thriving tourist industry—based on winter sports and cultural attractions such as historic Vienna and the famous Salzburg Festival—bolsters Austria's economy.

Austria's Alps, like those of France and Switzerland, attract thousands of winter sports enthusiasts every year.

Seven tiny states, two of them smaller than New York's Central Park, nestle among the larger countries of western Europe. They are a reminder of the turbulent history and countless boundary changes that have characterized Europe over the centuries.

Andorra

Status:	Co-principality
Area:	174 square miles
Population:	100,000
Capital:	Andorra la Vella
Languages:	Catalan, French, Spanish
Currency:	French franc (100 centimes) Spanish peseta (100 céntimos)

Monaco

Status:	Constitutional Monarchy
Area:	1.0 square mile
Population:	30,000
Capital:	Monaco
Languages:	French, Monegasque
Currency:	French franc (100 centimes)

Vatican City

Status:	Sovereign State of the Holy See
Area:	0.2 square miles
Population:	1,000
Capital:	Vatican City
Language:	Italian
Currency:	Italian lira (100 centisimos)

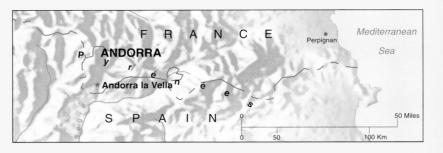

Andorra

Andorra sits on the French-Spanish border, high in the Pyrénées Mountains. Beginning in 1278, the Spanish Bishop of Urgel and the French Comte de Foix (later the French president) became the country's joint heads of state. When Andorra adopted its first constitution in 1993, these co-princes lost most of their power. An elected council with a modern constitution governs the country.

Tourism drives Andorra's economy. Visitors can buy Swiss watches, French wines, and many other luxury items without paying high **duties**. Andorra's few farmers graze sheep and goats on the mountain pastures and grow tobacco, potatoes, rye, and olives in the valleys.

Monaco

Tucked into the Mediterranean coast, Monaco lies nine miles east of the French city of Nice. The capital, also named Monaco, perches on a rocky headland, overlooking the Port of Monaco. Monte Carlo's casinos, luxury hotels, opera house, and famous beaches are just minutes away. Monegasques—natives of Monaco—comprise only 14 precent of the population. French citizens account for nearly half the population, and Italians number about 16 percent. The Grimaldi family has ruled Monaco since 1308, but in the past it accepted protection from and partial control by Italy, France, and Sardinia. Modern Monaco is an independent country with close ties to France.

Some Monegasques work in light industry, but Monaco's economy depends on tourism and banking. Extremely low taxes have encouraged foreign corporations to relocate to Monaco, and many of the world's wealthy and famous people have built lavish homes along the sun-drenched coast.

Vatican City

The walled enclosure of Vatican City lies on the west bank of the Tiber River in the middle of the city of Rome, Italy. The Vatican is the home of the Holy See—the Roman Catholic Church's governing body. Vatican City is also one of the world's great cultural treasure houses, containing museums, galleries, libraries, St. Peter's Basilica, and the Vatican Palace where Michelangelo's famous paintings grace the ceiling of the Sistine Chapel. The pope is head of state, but Vatican City also has a civil administration run by a governor and a Pontifical Commission. Popes have lived in the Vatican since the fifth century, except for a short period in the fourteenth century when they were based in Avignon, France.

Vatican City is all that remains of the **Papal States**, which once occupied most of central Italy and were ruled by the pope. In 1870 the Papal States became part of the Kingdom of Italy, and in 1929 Italy finally recognized the Vatican as an independent sovereign state.

San Marino

Status:	Republic
Area:	23 square miles
Population:	30,000
Capital:	San Marino
Language:	Italian
Currency:	Italian lira (100 centisimos)

San Marino

San Marino, the world's oldest republic, nestles on top of Mount Titano, a limestone peak on the eastern edge of the Apennine Mountains about 12 miles southwest of the Italian port of Rímini. Documents written in the eighth century mention a castle on Mount Titano, but some historians believe San Marino dates as far back as the fourth century A.D.

Many San Marinese work in tourism, hosting two million visitors each year. Other locals labor on small farms, in limestone quarries, or in factories producing leather goods, ceramics, and textiles.

Malta

Status:	Republic
Area:	124 square miles
Population:	400,000
Capital:	Valletta
Languages:	Maltese, English
Currency:	Maltese lira (100 cents)

Malta

The tiny island country of Malta, 60 miles south of Sicily, comprises three inhabited islands—Malta, Gozo, and Comino—and three small uninhabited islands. Formerly a British colony, Malta became independent in 1964.

Low limestone hills cover most of Malta. The soil is thin and dry, and farmers can raise only small crops of barley, wheat, potatoes, grapes, and citrus fruits. The Maltese have to import most of their food and also the fuel and raw materials for the islands' manufacturing industries—ship repairs, textiles, and electrical goods. Most Maltese work in the shipyards, in construction, or in tourism—Malta's fastest-growing industry. With its sunny climate, rocky cliffs, sandy beaches, and a wealth of historic and archaeological sites, Malta attracts visitors from all over the world.

Liechtenstein

Status:	Constitutional Monarchy
Area:	62 square miles
Population:	30,000
Capital:	Vaduz
Language:	German
Currency:	Swiss franc (100 centimes)

Luxembourg

Status:	Constitutional Monarchy
Area:	1,000 square miles
Population:	400,000
Capital:	Luxembourg
Languages:	French, German, Letzeburgish
Currency:	Luxembourg franc (100 centimes)

Liechtenstein

Roughly the size of Washington, D.C., Liechtenstein lies between Austria and Switzerland. A narrow strip of fertile land in the country's northwest runs along the Rhine River. Farmers use this lowland area to raise beef and dairy cattle and to grow grains, vegetables, and fruits—including grapes for wine production. Southeastern Liechtenstein is mountainous and nearly covered with pine forests. Before World War II, Liechtenstein was a farming country. The modern economy is highly industrialized, specializing in machinery, scientific and medical instruments, pharmaceuticals, ceramics, and textiles.

In the Middle Ages (A.D. 500 to A.D. 1500), Liechtenstein consisted of two states, Vaduz and Schellenberg. An Austrian prince named Johann-Adam Liechtenstein bought them in 1719. From 1815 to 1866 the country was part of the German Confederation but kept its independence. Liechtenstein remains a monarchy, ruled by the House of Liechtenstein, but also has a constitution and an elected government.

Luxembourg

The Grand Duchy of Luxembourg shares borders with Belgium, France, and Germany. Wooded hills in the north merge with the Belgian Ardennes. Fertile lowlands in the southern two-thirds of the country provide rich agricultural land where farmers grow barley, wheat, oats, and potatoes and raise pigs and cattle. Luxembourg's main industries are located in the south. Iron ore supplies the primary raw material for a huge iron and steel industry. Luxembourg's workforce also produces chemicals, plastics, synthetic fibers, and computer equipment.

Luxembourg was a founding member of the EU. The country also headquarters both the European Court of Justice and the European Coal and Steel Community. Luxembourg's history traces back to the Holy Roman Empire of the Middle Ages and includes periods of rule by Spain, Austria, France, and the Netherlands. The country gained its independence in 1867.

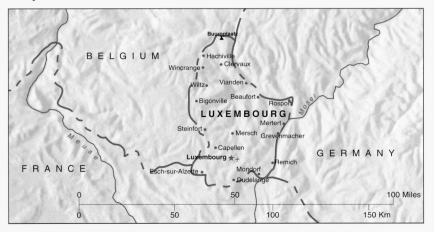

Italy

Italy

Status:	Republic
Area:	116,320 sq. miles
Population:	57.7 million
Capital:	Rome
Language:	Italian
Currency:	Italian lira (100 centesimi)

Italy's distinctive long, boot-shaped peninsula stretches 685 miles southward from the Alps to the Mediterranean Sea, reaching almost to the northern coast of Africa. Italy shares borders with France, Switzerland, Austria, and Slovenia and is bound by three seas—the Tyrrhenian Sea to the west, the Ionian Sea in the south, and the Adriatic Sea on the east. Italy's territory also includes the large islands of Sardinia to the west and Sicily, just off the toe of the boot.

The Alps in the far north provide Italy with magnificent scenery and fine skiing resorts that support a thriving winter tourist industry. Alpine rivers supply hydroelectric power to the large northwestern industrial centers of Milan, Turin, and Genoa. Just south of the mountains, the land levels out onto the North Italian Plain—Italy's only large lowland area. Farmers in this fertile region grow wheat, barley, rice, vegetables, fruits, and tobacco. The Po River and its **tributaries** provide the extra water needed to irrigate the rice fields in summer. Large numbers of tourists visit Venice and Verona in the northeast and Bologna and Florence farther south in the Apennine foothills.

The Apennine Mountains snake down the peninsula like a backbone, curving from west to east and back again. Italy's highest northern mountains run along the country's Adriatic shore. Broad coastal plains lie to the west. Farther south the mountains hug the Tyrrhenian coast, creating spectacular cliffs and headlands south of Naples. Historic Rome, the ruins of the ancient cities of Pompeii and Herculaneum, the Bay of Naples, and the island of Capri attract thousands of tourists to Italy's western coast. Italy also boasts Europe's only active volcanoes—Vesuvius just inland from Naples, Mount Etna on Sicily, and Stromboli and Vulcano on small islands off the north coast of Sicily.

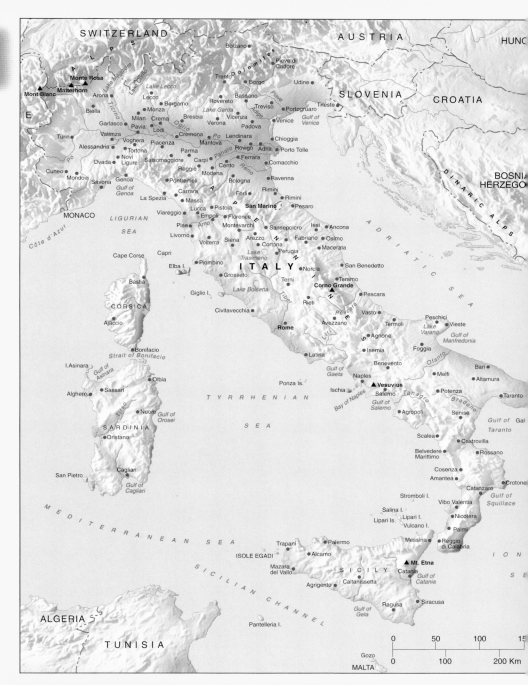

Italy

Southern Italy has a hotter, drier climate than the north. Most of the farmers are smallholders or tenants working farm plots on large estates. They graze sheep and goats on the dry uplands and grow olives, grapes, tomatoes, fruits, vegetables, and flowers—most of which they export to northern Europe.

Italians mine sulfur and mercury, and the quarries at Carrara produce some of the world's finest marble, but the country imports most industrial raw materials, fuel oil, and coal. Italian power is 80 percent thermal and 20 percent hydroelectric. Major iron and steel centers have developed in Taranto, Naples, Piombino, and Genoa. Italians manufacture vehicles, motorcycles, aircraft, ships, military equipment, power tools, electronic goods, household appliances, and textiles—especially fashion and sportswear. Petrochemical plants produce industrial chemicals, fertilizers, plastics, synthetic fibers, and rubber.

Poland

Poland

Status:	Republic
Area:	124,807 sq. miles
Population:	38.7 million
Capital:	Warsaw
Language:	Polish
Currency:	Zloty (100 groszy)

Poland's landscape is dominated by the Great North European Plain, a vast expanse of flat land extending from northern Germany, across Poland, and into neighboring Belarus and Ukraine. Soil quality is poor in northern Poland, and forests cover much of the countryside. Bialowieza National Park on the Polish–Belarussian border protects one of the last undisturbed ancient forests in Europe. Rich soil and the country's major farming regions lie in central and southern Poland. The Sudetic and Carpathian Mountains form Poland's jagged southern border.

Most Polish farms are small family businesses. Not highly mechanized, the farms cover almost two-thirds of the land, producing huge quantities of rye and potatoes. Lesser crops include barley, oats, wheat, sugar beets, and other vegetables. Many farmers also raise pigs, beef and dairy cattle, and sheep.

Poland's only coastline is a short expanse on the Baltic Sea with a well-developed fishing industry. Primary catches are cod and herring, much of which is processed in the ports of Szczecin, Gdańsk, and Gdynia—either frozen or canned for human consumption or turned into animal feed. The ports house ship repair yards, container terminals, and bulk cargo facilities for handling exports of coal, grain, and metal ores.

Southern Poland sits on one of the world's most abundant reserves of

hard coal and lignite, a soft brown coal. Polish workers also mine copper, silver, lead, zinc, and nickel. Iron and steel production in Katowice forms the backbone of Poland's industrial sector. Metal-based industries include ships, cars, aircraft, and railroad stock. Lódź is the hub of the country's textile industry, and Plock, near Warsaw, is the center of Poland's petrochemical industry.

The small family farms of central and southern Poland look much as they did a hundred years ago. The owner of this farm is growing grain and root crops, chiefly as feed for pigs and chickens.

Czech Republic, Slovakia, Hungary

Czech Republic

Status:	Republic
Area:	30,448 square miles
Population:	10.3 million
Capital:	Prague
Language:	Czech
Currency:	Koruna (100 haléru)

From 1918 to 1992, the Czech Republic was part of the Communist country of Czechoslovakia. Communist rule ended in 1989 when Václav Havel, a playwright, led the nonviolent Velvet Revolution, which toppled the old regime. In its place the Czech people adopted a democratic system with an elected government. The two factions of the old state—the Czechs and the Slovaks—could not agree on how to proceed, and on January 1, 1993, they separated into two nations called the Czech Republic and Slovakia. Good health and educational services enable the two states to have a higher standard of living than many of the former Communist states.

The Czech Republic is divided into the highland region of Bohemia in the west and the Moravian lowlands in the east. Farmers in both areas produce wheat, sugar beets, rye, hops, potatoes, and other vegetables. Summers are warm, but the winters are long and cold. Bohemian highlanders mine hard coal and lignite. Once the country's primary energy source, lignite is being replaced by cleaner energy forms. Mines in the highlands also produce uranium, lead, zinc, copper, mercury, and tin. Czech factories produce steel, machinery, cars, clothing, and leather goods, much of which is exported to western Europe.

Slovakia

Status:	Republic
Area:	18,923 square miles
Population:	5.4 million
Capital:	Bratislava
Languages:	Slovak, Hungarian, Czech
Currency:	Koruna (100 halierov)

Slovakia comprised the eastern one-third of Czechoslovakia until the two countries gained independence in 1993. The forested Carpathian Mountains dominate northern Slovakia. The rest of the country is mainly lowland, sloping south to east to merge with the Hungarian Plain. Several of Slovakia's rivers flow into the Danube, which marks the country's border with Hungary.

Slovakia's climate is temperate, with cold winters and hot summers, especially in the lowland areas. Farmers tend grains, beets, potatoes, and other vegetables. Pigs are common farm animals, as they are in many eastern European countries, but Slovak farmers also raise beef and dairy cattle, sheep, and poultry. Slovakia's main natural resources are iron ore, copper, lead, zinc, mercury, and perlite—a volcanic rock that is crushed and used to make plaster, cement, and some types of insulation. Factory workers make vehicles, machinery, chemicals, plastics, and paper. Coal-burning and hydroelectric power plants provide the country's energy.

Left: Prague, straddling the Vltava River, is one of Europe's oldest and most beautiful cities. The Charles Bridge, lined with statues of the Christian saints, is a local attraction in this City of a Hundred Spires.

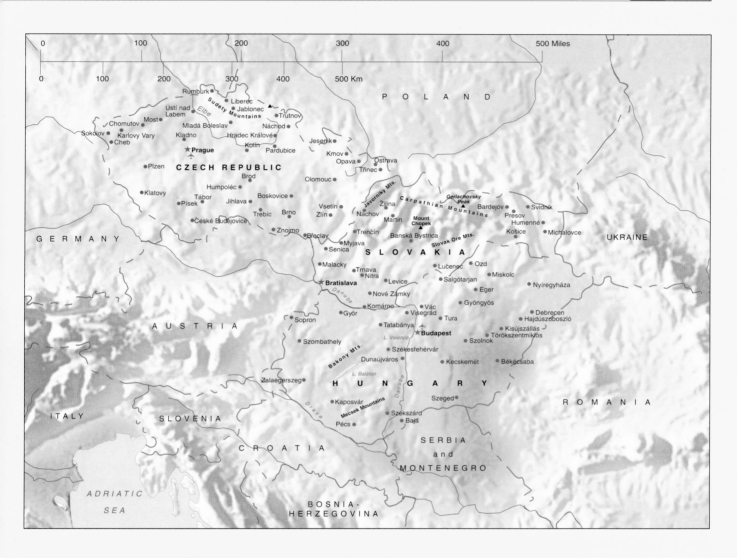

Hungary

Status:	Republic
Area:	35,919 square miles
Population:	10.1 million
Capital:	Budapest
Languages:	Hungarian, German
Currency:	Forint (100 fillér)

Two large lowlands dominate the Hungarian landscape—the Little Plain in the northwest and the Great Plain in the southeast. A line of low hills separates the two plains, stretching from Lake Balaton and the Bakony Forest to the Northern Highlands on the Hungarian-Slovakian border. At 45 miles long, Lake Balaton is central Europe's largest lake and a popular tourist resort.

Some of Europe's most fertile soil covers Hungary's plains, and the country's spring rains and long hot summers are ideal for growing wheat, corn, beets, potatoes and other vegetables. Upland farmers tend grapes for wine. Those in drier, sandy areas raise cattle, pigs, and poultry.

Factories in Hungary's main industrial regions around Budapest and Miskolc produce trucks and buses, machinery, chemicals, textiles, leather goods, and canned foods. Hungary has some natural gas and large deposits of bauxite—the principal ore of aluminum—but has to import most of the fuel and raw materials it needs for industry.

Slovenia, Croatia, Bosnia-Herzegovina

The Former Yugoslavia

Six republics comprised the former Yugoslavia until they split in 1991. Slovenia, Croatia, Macedonia, and Bosnia-Herzegovina quickly declared themselves independent republics. Serbia and Montenegro continued to call themselves Yugoslavia, although this term has only had partial acceptance. Throughout the 1990s, civil wars and ethnic conflicts plagued the region.

Events of the Conflict in the Former Yugoslavia

1990	Slovenia and Croatia hold the first multiparty elections in the Yugoslav republics. Macedonia and Bosnia-Herzegovina hold their own multiparty elections later in the year.
1991	Croatia and Slovenia declare independence. War breaks out between Croats and ethnic Serbs living in Croatian territory.
1992	In January, Macedonia declares independence. Bosnia-Herzegovina declares independence in April. Bosnian Muslims and Bosnian Croats begin fighting. Reports of ethnic cleansing of non-Serbs cause the UN to impose economic sanctions. Serbia and Montenegro form a new Yugoslavia.
1993	International negotiators present the Vance-Owen peace plan, which would divide Bosnia into ethnic provinces. The plan is rejected.
1994	Continued fighting provokes UN and NATO ultimatums; Bosnian Muslims agree to a truce with Bosnian Croats and the Croatian government. A cease-fire is negotiated.
1995	The cease-fire is broken six weeks early. In October, after thousands from both sides have been killed, all parties agree to a truce. The Dayton Peace agreement is signed in November. The United States and NATO agree to supply peacekeeping forces.
1997	Slobodan Milosevic becomes president of the federal republic of Yugoslavia (Serbia and Montenegro).
1998	In Kosovo, a Yugoslav province, Serbian police attempt to crack down on ethnic Albanians. In February, Yugoslav forces enter Kosovo. Under threat of NATO action, Yugoslav troops withdraw in October.
1999	After peace talks between Serbia and Kosovo fail, the UN begins an air strike against Yugoslavia. In May, Milosevic and others are indicted by the International Criminal Tribunal for the Former Yugoslavia (ICTY).

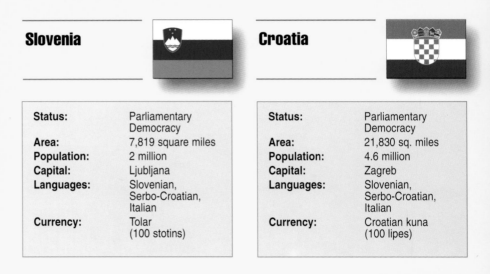

Slovenia

Status:	Parliamentary Democracy
Area:	7,819 square miles
Population:	2 million
Capital:	Ljubljana
Languages:	Slovenian, Serbo-Croatian, Italian
Currency:	Tolar (100 stotins)

Slovenia is a small mountainous country bordered by Italy, Austria, Hungary, and Croatia. It has a short stretch of Adriatic coastline to the southwest. Visitors are attracted to the country's mountain lakes, coastal resorts, limestone caves of Postojna (the largest European caverns), and the medieval capital, Ljubljana.

Slovenes farm about one-quarter of the land, growing grain, potatoes, beets, hops, flax, and fruit trees. Cattle, pigs, sheep, and horses graze on another one-quarter. About 40 percent of the country is covered in trees—conifers on the high ground, with chiefly beech and oak at the lower elevations. Swift rivers contribute hydroelectric power, and large deposits of coal provide fuel for thermal power plants. Slovenia's mines produce mercury, bauxite, copper, antimony, zinc, and iron ore. Manufactured goods include vehicles, chemicals, textiles, and electrical goods.

Croatia

Status:	Parliamentary Democracy
Area:	21,830 sq. miles
Population:	4.6 million
Capital:	Zagreb
Languages:	Slovenian, Serbo-Croatian, Italian
Currency:	Croatian kuna (100 lipes)

Croatia has two distinct climates split east to west along the Dinaric Alps. A large lowland region called the Pannonia Plains extends eastward to the Serbian border, and a contrasting region of limestone mountains extends southward along the coast. The Dinaric Alps and the resorts along the spectacular Dalmatian coast once attracted huge numbers of overseas visitors. Civil war has severely damaged this valuable tourist industry.

Thick black soil on Croatia's lowland plain provides some of the best farmland in Europe, producing large crops of grains, beets, cotton, sunflowers, olives, fruit, hemp, and flax. Local resources include coal, oil, natural gas, and bauxite. Before the civil war, Croatia's well-developed industries produced machinery, chemicals, cement, paper, lumber, electrical goods, and textiles. The people of Croatia are in the process of rebuilding their cities, industries, and **infrastructure**.

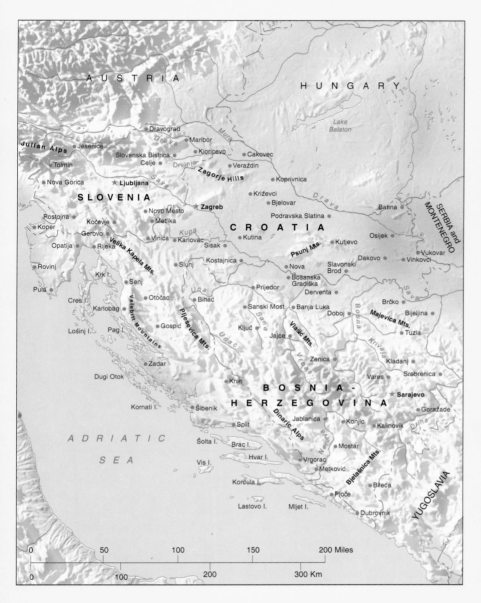

Above: Traditional crafts are still an important part of the local economy in rural parts of Croatia.

Below: A sheltered rocky inlet on Croatia's short Adriatic coastline.

Bosnia-Herzegovina

Status:	Democracy
Area:	19,741 sq. miles
Population:	3.8 million
Capital:	Sarajevo
Language:	Serbo-Croatian
Currency:	Marka (100 pfenniga)

Bosnia-Herzegovina borders Croatia to the west and north. Serbia is to the east, and Montenegro is to the south. The country is nearly landlocked, with just one 12-mile-long stretch of coast near the mouth of the Neretva River. The northern region, Bosnia, is mountainous and thickly forested. Herzegovina, the smaller southern section around the city of Mostar, consists of low hills and flat farmland. The country's coastal climate is mild, but the inland regions have short hot summers and bitterly cold winters with heavy snow.

Before the civil war, Bosnia had a thriving tourist industry of skiing, hunting, fishing, and river kayaking. Vast forests, large reserves of iron ore and coal, and abundant hydroelectric power enabled Bosnian industries to produce vehicles, machinery, textiles, and electrical goods. The country's farmers grew wheat, corn, fruits, vegetables, and tobacco. Much of Bosnia's industry and agriculture were devastated by the war, but efforts are under way to repair the damage.

Serbia, Montenegro, Macedonia

lower pastures, and sheep feed on the higher ground.

Serbian natural resources include oil, gas, coal, copper, lead, and zinc. Montenegrans mine bauxite, coal, and lead. Manufacturing industries are concentrated around Belgrade in the north and Cetinje and Podgorica in the south and output vehicles, military equipment, paper, plastics, cement, textiles, and electrical goods. Civil war and ethnic conflicts have raged since 1992 and have destroyed much of the area's agriculture and industry.

Macedonia

Status:	Republic
Area:	9,927 sq. miles
Population:	2 million
Capital:	Skopje
Language:	Macedonian
Currency:	Macedonian dinar (100 dari)

Serbia and Montenegro (Yugoslavia)

Status:	Republic
Area:	39,448 sq. miles
Population:	10.6 million
Capital:	Belgrade (Serbia) and Podgorica
Languages:	Serbo-Croatian, Albanian, Hungarian
Currency:	New dinar (100 paras)

Serbia and Montenegro are the two former republics of Yugoslavia that act as a joint independent state. The two countries have three contrasting landscapes. Fertile lowlands cover the northern part of Serbia. The plains drain into the Danube River, which flows east into neighboring Romania through a spectacular gorge called the Iron Gate. Central and southern Serbia are mountainous and include parts of the Dinaric Alps and the Balkan Mountains. Roughly one-quarter of Serbia is covered in forest—firs and pines on the mountain slopes, with oak and beech on the lower ground. The third region, Montenegro in the southwest, consists of a limestone plateau with typical **karst** scenery and shrub vegetation. The coastal region has hot, dry summers and cool winters. Inland, the climate is more extreme. The mountains have cool summers and very cold winters, while the northern plains have hot, dry summers and cold winters.

Farmland and pasture cover about half of Serbia and Montenegro. Corn, wheat, potatoes, and tobacco comprise the bulk of the crops, but many farmers grow olives, figs, grapes, pears, plums, and other fruits. Cattle and pigs graze on the

Macedonia is a country of wooded mountains, rising to 9,068 feet in the Korab range on the Albanian border. Most of the land is drained by the south-flowing Vardar River.

Ancient Macedonia included parts of Greece and Bulgaria and was the center of the great Kingdom of Macedonia. Macedonia was in turn part of the Roman, Byzantine, and Ottoman Empires. In 1945 Macedonia one of the six republics of Yugoslavia. Modern Macedonia declared its independence in 1991.

Macedonia's farmers supply most of the country's meat, dairy products, cereals, vegetables, and fruit. They grow cotton and tobacco for home use and for export. Mines produce a wide range of metal ores and some coal, but Macedonia depends on imported oil and gas to fuel its manufacturing industries.

Albania and Greece

Albania

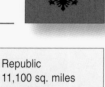

Status:	Republic
Area:	11,100 sq. miles
Population:	3.5 million
Capital:	Tiranë
Language:	Albanian
Currency:	Lek (100 qintars)

Greece

Status:	Parliamentary Republic
Area:	50,950 sq. miles
Population:	10.5 million
Capital:	Athens
Language:	Greek
Currency:	Drachma (100 leptas)

Mainland Greece occupies the ragged southern end of the Balkan Peninsula, which juts more than 300 miles into the Mediterranean Sea. The country is bordered by Albania, Macedonia, and Bulgaria in the north and by the Ionian Sea to the west. Turkey and the Aegean Sea lie to the east. Greece also includes more than 2,000 islands, most of them scattered across the Aegean side of the mainland. Some islands in the Dodecanese group lie barely 10 miles off the Turkish coast.

Albania is a small country on the Adriatic Sea, cut off from its neighbors by high, rugged, inland mountain ranges. The country has been conquered many times, and for nearly 500 years it was part of the Turkish Ottoman Empire. In 1912 Albania broke free from Turkish rule and declared its independence. From 1928 to 1939, Albania was a monarchy ruled by King Zog. After World War II, it became a Communist republic. In 1992 the Albanian people elected their first non-Communist president.

After years of isolation, Albania is attempting to modernize, but the change from a Communist system to a western-style economy is difficult. Albania is the poorest country in Europe. Most of the people are farmers, growing corn, grapes, sugar beets, olives, potatoes, and grains and raising livestock. Farming methods are often primitive. Few farmers have modern machinery, and many still use horses for plowing and pulling carts. Albania is reasonably rich in resources, yet the country's industries are poorly developed. Albanians mine oil, gas, bitumen (used for surfacing roads), copper, iron, nickel, and large reserves of chrome—the country's most lucrative export.

Fast-flowing mountain rivers generate hydroelectric power, and extensive hardwood and softwood forests supply the raw materials for lumber, plywood, pulp, and paper factories.

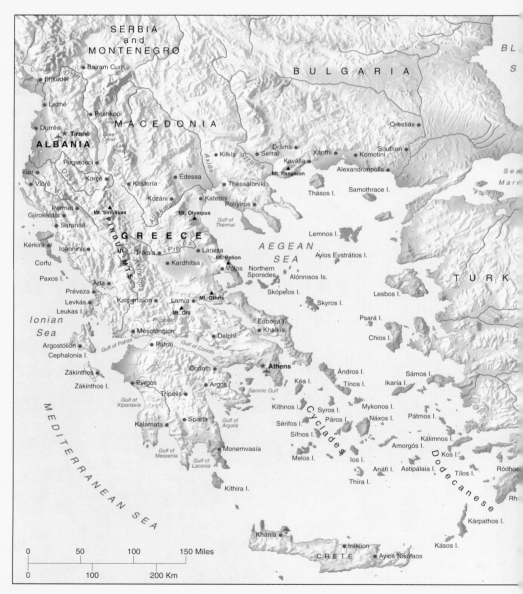

Greece

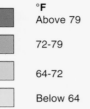

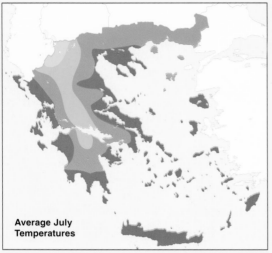

Average July Temperatures

°F
- Above 79
- 72-79
- 64-72
- Below 64

Greece's coastal regions and islands are very hot in summer, although temperatures are lower inland, especially in the mountains. In winter the coastal areas and islands are mild, generally above 40°F, while temperatures in the north central mountains fall to around zero—and often below.

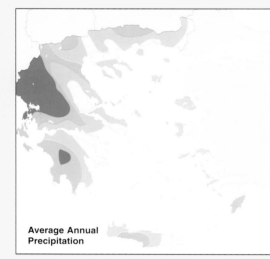

Average Annual Precipitation

Inches
- Above 40
- 32-40
- 24-32
- Below 24

Left: Prevailing westerly winds ensure that the western side of mainland Greece receives the most rain—40 inches and more compared with a meager 24 inches on the eastern side.

Below: Byzantine buildings overlook the sea at Monemvasia on the Aegean coast—one of the southernmost towns of mainland Greece.

Crete is the largest island, at 3,200 square miles. More than half a million people live on Crete. With their Mediterranean climate, picturesque villages, spring flowers, and beautiful scenery and beaches, the Greek islands attract more than 10 million tourists each year.

Greece is mostly dry, scrub-covered mountains, rising to 8,256 feet in the northwest. Mount Olympus, famous from Greek mythology, towers over the eastern central portion of the country, reaching 9,573 feet. Narrow strips of lowland follow the coast, and several small fertile valleys dot the Macedonia and Thrace regions north of the Aegean Sea. Most Greeks live near the coast and have done so for generations. The country's numerous inlets and bays support Greece's long tradition as a seafaring nation. The country has one of the world's largest merchant fleets, and shipping is a significant source of income.

Greece produces small amounts of bauxite, lead, zinc, chrome, nickel, and silver, but the country does not have the large energy resources needed for **smelting**, so most of the ore is exported. Farming provides the bulk of jobs and income. Farmers grow wheat, corn, tomatoes, olives, grapes, citrus fruits, cotton, and tobacco. Food processing plants create canned olives, olive oil, and dried grapes (sultanas and raisins) for export.

Romania

Romania

Status:	Republic
Area:	92,042 sq. miles
Population:	22.5 million
Capital:	Bucharest
Language:	Romanian
Currency:	Leu
	(100 bani)

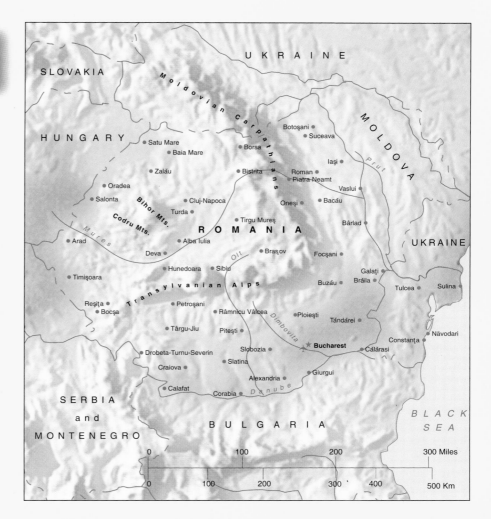

Romania, like many of its neighbors, has recently become a democratic republic after more than 50 years of Communism—24 of them under the rule of Nicolae Ceausescu. In 1989 the Romanian people, backed by the army, overthrew Ceausescu's regime in a short but violent revolution. The people adopted a new constitution in 1991.

Romania is a mountainous country, but the elevations are not so extreme as to inhibit travel. The Transylvanian Plateau in the country's center consists of rolling hills and fertile farmland 1,000 feet to 2,000 feet above sea level. Around it a great arc of mountains, the Moldovian Carpathians and the Transylvanian Alps, snakes south from the Ukrainian border and then goes westward into Serbia. The lower Bihor Mountains in the northwest complete the highland ring encircling the plateau. Outside the mountain ring, lowlands stretch clear to the country's borders. The western lowlands merge with the plains of Serbia and Hungary. The eastern plains slope down to the Black Sea and include the marshes and lakes along the lower Danube River.

The fertile soil of the central plateau and plains provides abundant grains, beets, oilseeds, fruits, and vegetables. Farmers with rich pastures raise pigs, sheep, and dairy cattle. Romania produces enough food for local needs and exports surplus grains, fruits, and wine to neighboring countries. Forests cover about one-quarter of the land, providing raw materials for house and furniture construction and for the paper industries. Hydroelectric power and natural gas supply much of the nation's energy, but Romania also imports coal and oil. The country's mineral resources include copper, lead, zinc, aluminum ore, and sulfur. Factories concentrated around Bucharest in the south make vehicles, machinery, textiles, furniture, and food products.

Above: One of the many heavy-industry complexes concentrated around the Romanian capital, Bucharest, in the extreme southeast of the country

Bulgaria

Bulgaria

Status:	Republic
Area:	42,822 sq. miles
Population:	8.2 million
Capital:	Sofia
Language:	Bulgarian
Currency:	Lev
	(100 stotinki)

East-west bands of lowlands and mountains separate Bulgaria into four distinct land regions. The fertile Danube Valley stretches across northern Bulgaria. The Balkan Mountains march across the country's middle, rising to about 6,500 feet in the west and gradually descending toward the Black Sea. To the south lies the broad fertile Maritsa River Valley. And south of the Maritsa, the land rises again to the Rhodope Mountains, which separate Bulgaria from Greece and Turkey.

Hot summers and cold winters characterize the Danube Valley, where farmers grow wheat, barley, corn, beets, and vegetables. The Maritsa Valley is milder, with damp winters and warm, dry summers. Farmers in this region cultivate grapes, rice, sunflowers, grains, and tobacco. Bulgarian farmers produce more than just edible crops. The fragrant petals of the country's roses contain a sweet-smelling oil—attar of roses—that is sold to perfumeries all over the world.

Agriculture and tourism drive Bulgaria's economy. Mines in the Rhodope Mountains produce iron, copper, lead, and zinc, but Bulgaria is very short of fuel and has to import energy for its industries. Steel, machinery, cement, and textiles are the country's primary industrial products.

Left: Bright yellow fields of oilseed plants cover much of the Danube lowlands. More than half of Bulgaria's people earn their living from agriculture—one of the highest proportions in Europe.

Below: Workers gather the grape harvest from a hillside vineyard in the Maritsa Valley.

Belarus, Moldova, Ukraine

Belarus

Status:	Republic
Area:	80,154 sq. miles
Population:	10.2 million
Capital:	Minsk
Languages:	Belarussian, Russian
Currency:	Belarussian ruble (100 kopeks)

Belarus has changed hands often. The country was once part of the Mongol Empire, then a portion of Lithuania, then a section of Poland. In 1918 the country achieved its independence but was invaded by Russia the following year, becoming one of the original Soviet Union members. Belarus gained its independence again in 1991 but maintains close ties with Russia.

Most of Belarus is a vast, flat plain. A line of low hills runs through the middle of the country, but the highest point is only 112 feet above sea level.

Above: The main street in Smorgon, in northwestern Belarus

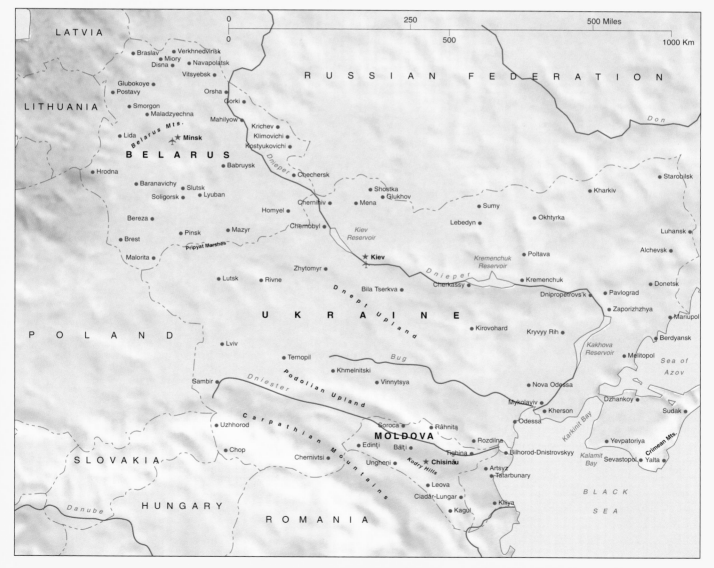

Belarus, Moldova, Ukraine

Southern Belarus contains Europe's largest area of marshes and peat bogs—the famous Pripyat Marshes. Forests cover about one-third of the land—birch and pine in the north, with ash, oak, and hornbeam in the warmer south.

Belarussian factories produce trucks and tractors, machinery, computers, household appliances, pulp, paper, fertilizers, and industrial chemicals. Belarus trades many of its goods to Russia, receiving energy supplies and raw materials in return. Farms cover nearly half of the country. Many farmers concentrate on cattle, pigs, sheep, and goats. The remainder grow grains, beets, potatoes, flax, and hemp.

Moldova

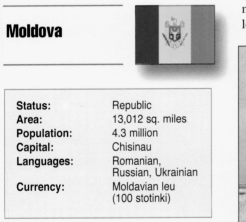

Status:	Republic
Area:	13,012 sq. miles
Population:	4.3 million
Capital:	Chisinau
Languages:	Romanian, Russian, Ukrainian
Currency:	Moldavian leu (100 stotinki)

Moldova is a small republic sandwiched between Ukraine and Romania. Most of the country is hilly, especially in the center where it rises to 1,400 feet. The hills give way to a broad flat plain in the south. Moldova has virtually no mineral resources and no oil or gas, but it has extremely fertile soil and a mild climate. As a result, Moldova's economy depends primarily on agriculture and on industries associated with farming, such as flour milling, food processing, wine making, brewing, and the manufacture of leather goods, cigarettes, textiles, soybean products, and sunflower oil.

Ukraine

Status:	Republic
Area:	233,089 sq. miles
Population:	49.9 million
Capital:	Kiev
Languages:	Ukrainian, Russian
Currency:	Hryvnia (100 kopiykas)

Covering more than 230,000 square miles, Ukraine is the largest country lying within Europe. Russia is bigger, but it stretches into northern Asia, so it spans two continents. Ukraine consists mainly of plains, called **steppes,** with low hills separating the major river valleys—the Dniester, the Bug, and the Dnieper, all of which flow into the Black Sea. Ukraine has few mountains. The Carpathians are far to the west, and the Crimean Mountains lie in the south.

Ukraine has abundant peat, coal, and natural gas but has to supplement its meager oil reserves with imports from neighboring countries. Its major industrial regions in the east and south house coal fields and iron ore mines. Ukraine is also one of the world's chief producers of manganese. Like many former states of the Soviet Union, Ukraine's industry was underdeveloped. Modern Ukrainian factories include chemicals, plastics, and food-processing plants. Odessa on the Black Sea is Ukraine's chief port and shipbuilding center.

Above: Ukraine's fertile lowlands produce about 8 percent of the world's barley and 12 percent of the world's sugar beets, but in 1986 huge tracts of farmland were contaminated by the reactor explosion at the Chernobyl nuclear power station.

Above: Modern apartments and offices in the center of Chisinau, Moldova

Above: The Dniester flows from the Carpathians across the lowlands of Ukraine.

Russian Federation (European Russia)

Russian Federation

Status:	Federation
Area:	6,592,819 sq. miles
Population:	146.5 million
Capital:	Moscow
Language:	Russian
Currency:	Russian ruble (100 kopeks)

Russia is the largest country in the world. Even after losing 14 of the 15 republics that comprised the former Soviet Union, Russia is still nearly twice the size of the United States. The Russian Federation stretches 6,000 miles from the borders of Norway, Finland, and the Baltic States in the west to the Pacific Ocean in the east. It extends almost 2,800 miles from the Arctic Ocean to the borders of Kazakhstan, Mongolia, and China.

Russia traces its history to the medieval Slavic state of Kievan Rus, which covered most of modern Ukraine, Belarus, and European Russia. Mongol invaders from central Asia destroyed Kievan Rus in the thirteenth century. In the 1300s, a new state called Muscovy took its place and was succeeded in the 1700s by the Russian Empire. The Russian Revolution of 1917 ended imperial rule, replacing it with a Communist government, which remained in power until 1991.

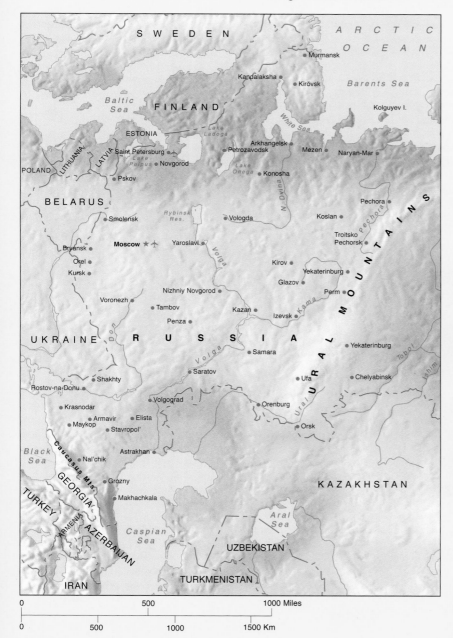

Above: European Russia—west of the Urals—is dwarfed by its eastern (Asian) segment. A train journey from Moscow to Vladivostok takes seven days and passes through eight time zones.

Above center: The cruiser Aurora on the Neva River that flows through Saint Petersburg

Above: Russians enjoy a traditional winter pastime—fishing through holes in the ice on a frozen lake at Zagorsk.

Russian Federation (European Russia)

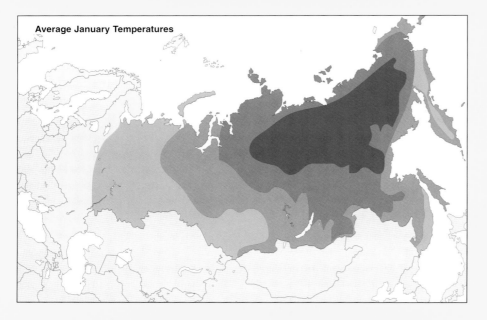

Average January Temperatures

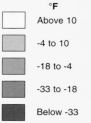

°F
- Above 10
- -4 to 10
- -18 to -4
- -33 to -18
- Below -33

Above and below: Russia experiences some of the coldest weather conditions on earth. In January, temperatures in eastern Siberia plunge as low as -90°F for weeks at a time. Only in the extreme west of the country do average winter temperatures remain above 10°F. Even in summer, the northern half of the country remains below 60°F. The only part of this vast land to receive any real summer warmth is the southwest, bordering the Black Sea and the Caspian Sea—Russia's favorite vacation area.

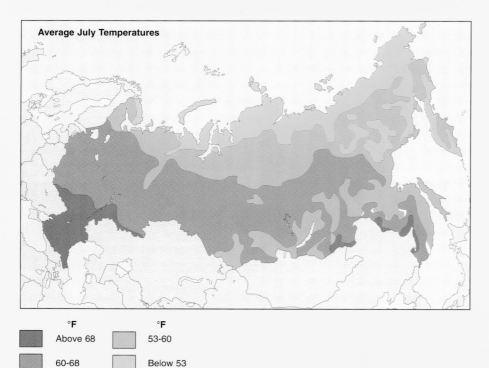

Average July Temperatures

°F
- Above 68
- 60-68

°F
- 53-60
- Below 53

During the 1990s, Russians suffered great hardships. The country tried to change from the Communist system—under which the government controlled everything—to a free-market economy where people can own their own companies and compete with one another for business.

Russia's vast land area consists of four main regions—the European Plain (European Russia), which extends as far as the Ural Mountains; the West Siberian Plain between the Urals and the Yenisey River; the Central Siberian Plateau between the Yenisey and Lena Rivers; and the East Siberian Highlands.

Most of European Russia lies on the European Plain, bounded by the Carpathian and Caucasus Mountains in the south and by the Urals in the east. Mount Elbrus is Russia's highest peak at 18,510 feet. Climate and vegetation vary greatly from north to south. Treeless tundra dominates the Arctic zone. South of the tundra lies a forested belt of pine, spruce, and fir called the **taiga**, which merges southward into mixed forests of birch, oak, elm, and maple. Fishing and herding reindeer are traditional occupations in these harsh northern regions. In the forested zones, farmers grow potatoes and flax and raise livestock. The steppes stretch across the southern part of the country, containing the rich black and brown soil that makes Russia the world's foremost producer of barley, oats, wheat, and rye. Farmers in the warmer southern region bordering Ukraine and the Black Sea grow a variety of vegetables, as well as subtropical crops such as tea and citrus fruits.

Large coal fields operate near the capital city of Moscow, in the northern Urals, and on the Russian-Ukrainian border. Oil fields in the Urals, the Arctic, and the Caucasus Mountains provide fuel and raw materials for Russia's petrochemical industries. Huge iron ore deposits along the Ukrainian border support the country's iron and

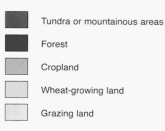

- Tundra or mountainous areas
- Forest
- Cropland
- Wheat-growing land
- Grazing land

Right: Russia is enormously rich in natural resources. Thousands of square miles of forest yield lumber, pulp, and paper. Fast-flowing rivers provide hydropower. Huge mineral reserves feed the nation's industries. Fertile black soils in the southwest make Russia the world's leading grain producer.

Below: Moscow at midnight. On the left, the clock tower marks one of the main gates in the wall of the Kremlin complex. On the right, spectacular onion domes crown Saint Basil's Cathedral in Red Square. And in the distance, at the far side of Red Square, stands the imposing facade of the State Historical Museum.

Land Use in Russia

St. Petersburg
Moscow
Nizhni Novgorod
Kursk
Volograd

steel industries. Russia also has vast reserves of most other minerals, but many are located in remote areas, far from European Russia's manufacturing centers, which are located in Saint Petersburg, Moscow, Kursk, Nizhny Novgorod, and Volgograd. To compensate, Russia imports fuel and raw materials from many of the states along its western borders.

Glossary

alluvial plain: a level tract of land bordering a river on which sediment has been deposited

drumlin: a long, oval-shaped hill or ridge made of finely ground rocks

duties: taxes paid to a government on goods brought in from another country

fjord: a long, narrow sea inlet bordered by steep cliffs

fodder crops: coarse plants—such as cornstalks, hay, and straw—that are grown as food for cattle, horses, and other farm animals

glacier: a large body of ice and snow that moves slowly over land

heathland: an area of open land covered by heather, low shrubs, and other hardy vegetation

ice age: an ancient period when ice sheets covered large regions of the earth. The last ice age—the Pleistocene—ended about 10,000 years ago.

infrastructure: the basic system of public works (schools, hospitals, highways, docks, railways, etc.) that enable a country, state, or region to live and work

karst: a limestone region with underground streams and caverns

Massif Central: the plateau region of south central France that reaches to more than 6,000 feet above sea level

meseta: an extensive, heavily eroded plateau area of Spain's interior that covers about three-quarters of the country and that is crossed by several mountain ranges

moor: a wild stretch of usually elevated land that is covered with heather, coarse grass, and other hardy vegetation

nationality: a group of people who, because they share race, language, tradition, and origin, can be distinguished from other populations

Papal States: lands, mostly in central Italy, that were once under the economic, military, and political rule of the Roman Catholic popes. In modern times, the pope governs only Vatican City.

polder: an area of land that has been reclaimed from the sea. The land is enclosed in a series of protective boundaries and is then drained by pumping the water into canals.

population density: the size of a population divided by land area, usually measured by the number of people who live in a square mile. The more people who live in the square mile, the denser the population is said to be.

smelting: the act of melting to get the pure metal of certain minerals or ores to separate away from the waste matter

steppes: the level, generally treeless grasslands of Russia and southern Europe

taiga: the belt of forested land lying to the south of the tundra. The trees in the taiga are mostly cone-bearing evergreens, such as spruces and firs.

tributary: a river that joins a larger river

tundra: a region of treeless plains and permanently frozen soil around the Arctic Circle

Index